SRA

Reading Mastery

Plus

Language Arts Guide

Level 3

Siegfried Engelmann
Susan Hanner

SRA

A Division of The McGraw-Hill Companies

Columbus, Ohio

Illustration Credits
Susan Jerde

www.sra4kids.com

SRA/McGraw-Hill

*A Division of The **McGraw·Hill** Companies*

Send all inquiries to:
SRA/McGraw-Hill
8787 Orion Place
Columbus, OH 43240-4027

Printed in the United States of America.

ISBN 0-07-569135-3

4 5 6 7 8 9 DBH 06 05 04

Table of Contents

Lesson 51

Materials: Each student will need a copy of the worksheet for lesson 51 (blackline master 1) and a copy of textbook B.

TABLE OF CONTENTS

Name _____

Lesson 51

1. What part of your textbook shows a list of the selections in the book, starting with page 1? _____

2. What is the title of the selection for lesson 74? _____

3. On what page does the selection for lesson 74 begin? _____

4. What is the title of the selection for lesson 85? _____

5. On what page does that selection begin? _____

a. (Write on the board:)

table of contents

- You're going to learn about the table of contents. The table of contents is at the beginning of your textbook. (Hold up textbook B and show the Table of Contents.)

b. The table of contents is a list of selections that are in the textbook. The order of the list is based on the page number. The first thing on the list shows the selection that starts on page 2 in the textbook. The next thing on the list shows the next selection in the program and it shows the page number on which the selection begins.

c. Your turn: Open your book to the beginning of the book and find the Table of Contents. (Observe students and give feedback.)

- Everybody, touch the first title on the list.✔

- Read the title of the first selection in this book. (Call on a student.) *The Air Around the Earth.*

- On what page does that selection begin? (Call on a student.) *1.*

- Read the title of the next selection in this book. (Call on a student.) *Herman Flies to Italy.*

- On what page number does that selection begin? (Call on a student.) *2.*

d. Right before the titles of the selections are lesson numbers. Everybody, touch lesson number 65.

- Everybody, what's the title of the selection for lesson 65? (Signal.) *The City of Troy.*

e. New problem. Listen: What selection will you read in lesson 76? Find lesson 76 in the Table of Contents and raise your hand when you know the title of the selection. ✔

- Everybody, what's the selection for lesson 76? (Signal.) *Inside a Hot Van.*

- The table of contents shows the page on which that selection begins. Raise your hand when you know the first page of the selection, *Inside a Hot Van.* ✔

- Everybody, on what page does it begin? (Signal.) *209.*

f. New problem: Raise your hand when you know the selection you will read in lesson 68. ✔

- Everybody, what's the title of the selection for lesson 68? (Signal.) *Bertha Has a Great Sense of Smell.*

- Everybody, look at the page number of the beginning of the selection and turn to that page. Be careful because there are two numbers at the bottom of the page. One is a lesson number. You want to find the **page** number. Raise your hand when you've turned to the page

51

for the selection, *Bertha Has a Great Sense of Smell.*

(Observe students and give feedback.)

- Everybody, what page number is your textbook opened to? (Signal.) *156.*
- Hold up your textbook and show me page 156. ✔

g. Find lesson 51 on your worksheet. ✔

- These are questions about some of the things we just went over. Follow along while I read. Item 1. What part of your textbook shows a list of the selections in the book, starting with page 1? Everybody, what's the answer? (Signal.) *The table of contents.*
- Later you'll look at the table of contents and answer the following questions: Item 2. What is the title of the selection for lesson 74?

Item 3. On what page does the selection for lesson 74 begin?
Item 4. What is the title of the selection for lesson 85?
Item 5. On what page does that selection begin?

h. (Tell students when they should complete the items.)

i. (After students complete the items, do a workcheck. For each item: Read the item. Call on a student to answer it. If the answer is wrong, say the correct answer.)

Answer Key: 1. Table of contents **2.** *Bertha Tests Some Water* **3.** 195 **4.** *Cave Pictures* **5.** 275

Lesson 52

TABLE OF CONTENTS

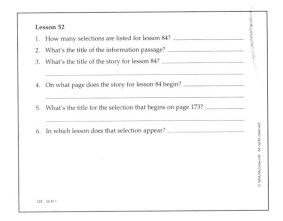

a. At the beginning of your textbook is a list of all selections that are in the textbook. Everybody, what's the name of that list? (Signal.) *Table of contents.*

b. Your turn: Open your book to the beginning and find the Table of Contents. (Observe students and give feedback.)

c. Listen: You're going to read a selection that begins on page 108. Look down the page number column until you come to page 108. Raise your hand when you've done that much. ✔

• Everybody, what's the title of the selection you'll read on page 108? (Signal.) *Landing a Ship.*

• Raise your hand when you know the lesson number for that selection. ✔

• Everybody, what lesson number? (Signal.) *63.*

d. New problem. Find the title of the selection that starts on page 148. (Observe students and give feedback.)

• Everybody, what's the title? (Signal.) *The Great Wooden Horse.*

• Everybody, what's the lesson number for that selection? (Signal.) *67.*

e. Some of the lessons have more than one selection. They have an information passage and a story. Find out what you'll read in lesson 55. (Observe students and give feedback.)

• You'll read two selections on that lesson.

• Everybody, what's the title of the first selection? (Signal.) *Facts About Islands.*

• That's the information passage.

• What's the title of the story for lesson 55? (Signal.) *Linda and Kathy Find Land.*

f. Find lesson 52 on your worksheet. ✔

• Follow along while I read the items. Item 1. How many selections are listed for lesson 84? Item 2. What's the title of the information passage? Item 3. What's the title of the story for lesson 84? Item 4. On what page does the story for lesson 84 begin? Item 5. What's the title for the selection that begins on page 173? Item 6. In which lesson does that selection appear?

g. (Tell the students when they should complete the items.)

h. (After the students complete the items, do a workcheck. For each item: Read the item. Call on a student to answer it. If the answer is wrong, say the correct answer.)

Answer Key: 1. 2 **2.** *Fire and Heat* **3.** *The Cave People Discover Fire* **4.** 267 **5.** *Oil Wells* **6.** 71

Lesson 53

Materials: Each student will need a copy of the worksheet for lesson 53 (blackline master 2) and a copy of textbook B.

SUBJECT—VERB AGREEMENT

Lesson 53

A. Write **one** or **more than one** after each sentence. Write **jump** or **jumps** in each blank.

1. The girl _____. _____

2. You and I _____. _____

3. Cats and dogs _____. _____

4. Those frogs _____. _____

5. A man _____. _____

6. Mark and Henry _____. _____

B.

1. How many selections are listed for lesson 81? _____

2. What's the page number for the first selection in lesson 81? _____

3. What's the page number for the second selection in lesson 81? _____

4. What's the title of the second selection? _____

---

a. (Write on the board:)

jump   jumps

- (Point to **jump**.)
  Here's a rule about when to say verbs like **jump.** Listen. When you're talking about **more than one** thing, you say **jump.**
- Everybody, when do you say **jump?** (Signal.) *When you're talking about more than one thing.*
- (Repeat until firm.)

b. (Point to **jump**.)
  You also say **I jump** and **you jump.** What do you also say? (Signal.) *I jump and you jump.*

c. (Point to **jumps**.)
  Here's a rule about when to say verbs like **jumps.** This rule is true except when you say **I jump** or **you jump.** Listen. When you're talking about one thing, you say **jumps.**
- When do you say **jumps?** (Signal.) *When you're talking about one thing.*
- (Repeat until firm.)

d. Remember, if you're talking about one, you say **jumps.** If you're talking about more than one, you say **jump.**
- Everybody, what do you say if you're talking about one? (Signal.) *Jumps.*
- What do you say if you're talking about more than one? (Signal.) *Jump.*
- (Repeat until firm.)

e. When you say **Sue,** are you talking about **one** or **more than one?** (Signal.) *One.*
- So do you say **jump** or **jumps?** (Signal.) *Jumps.*
- When you say **Sue and Randy,** are you talking about **one** or **more than one?** (Signal.) *More than one.*
- So do you say **jump** or **jumps?** (Signal.) *Jump.*

f. When you say **Juan,** are you talking about **one** or **more than one?** (Signal.) *One.*
- So do you say **jump** or **jumps?** (Signal.) *Jumps.*
- When you say **cats,** are you talking about **one** or **more than one?** (Signal.) *More than one.*
- So do you say **jump** or **jumps?** (Signal.) *Jump.*
- When you say **Sandra and the cats,** are you talking about **one** or **more than one?** (Signal.) *More than one.*
- So do you say **jump** or **jumps?** (Signal.) *Jump.*
- (Repeat step f until firm.)

g. I'll say sentences that have a **blank** in them. Tell me if the word **jump** or the word **jumps** goes in the blank.

h. Listen. Cats and dogs **blank.** Everybody, what word? (Signal.) *Jump.*
- Say the sentence with **jump.** (Signal.) *Cats and dogs jump.*
- Listen. You and I **blank.** Everybody, what word? (Signal.) *Jump.*
- Say the sentence. (Signal.) *You and I jump.*
- Listen. The girl **blank.** Everybody, what word? (Signal.) *Jumps.*
- Say the sentence. (Signal.) *The girl jumps.*
- (Repeat step h until firm.)

i. Listen. The women **blank.** Everybody, what word? (Signal.) *Jump.*
- Say the sentence. (Signal.) *The women jump.*
- Listen. A man **blank.** Everybody, what word? (Signal.) *Jumps.*
- Say the sentence. (Signal.) *A man jumps.*
- Listen. Mark and Aaron **blank.** Everybody, what word? (Signal.) *Jump.*
- Say the sentence. (Signal.) *Mark and Aaron jump.*
- Listen. Those frogs **blank.** Everybody, what word? (Signal.) *Jump.*
- Say the sentence. (Signal.) *Those frogs jump.*
- (Repeat step i until firm.)

j. Find part A on your worksheet. ✔
- These are the sentences we just did. You'll write **one** or **more than one** after each sentence. You'll write **jump** or **jumps** in each blank.

k. (Tell the students when they should complete the items in parts A and B.)

l. (After the students complete the items, do a workcheck. For each item: Read the item. Call on a student to answer it. If the answer is wrong, say the correct answer.)

Answer Key: Part A: 1. jumps; one
2. jump; more than one **3.** jump; more than one **4.** jump; more than one **5.** jumps; one
6. jump; more than one
Part B: 1. 2 **2.** 240 **3.** 241 **4.** *The Greatest Soldier*

Lesson 54

Materials: Each student will need a copy of the worksheet for lesson 54 (blackline master 3) and a copy of textbook B.

SUBJECT—VERB AGREEMENT

Lesson 54

A. Write **one** or **more than one** after each sentence. Write **run** or **runs** in each blank.

1. This woman _____. _____
2. Boys and girls _____. _____
3. She _____. _____
4. Her pals _____. _____
5. Her pal _____. _____
6. Two men _____. _____

B.

1. What's the lesson number for the selection that begins on page 91?

   _____

2. What's the title of the selection that begins on page 91?

   _____

3. What's the lesson number for the selection that begins on page 216?

   _____

4. What's the title of the selection that begins on page 216?

   _____

---

a. (Write on the board:)

run   runs

- (Point to **run**.)
  Here's a rule about when to say verbs like **run**. Listen. When you're talking about **more than one** thing, you say **run.**
- Everybody, when do you say **run?** (Signal.) *When you're talking about more than one thing.*
- (Repeat until firm.)

b. (Point to **run**.)
  You also say **I run** and **you run**. What do you also say? (Signal.) *I run and you run.*

c. (Point to **runs**.)
  Here's a rule about when to say verbs like **runs**. This rule is true **except** when you say **I run** or **you run**. Listen.
- When you're talking about **one** thing, you say **runs.**
- When do you say **runs?** (Signal.) *When you're talking about one thing.*
- (Repeat until firm.)

- Remember, if you're talking about one, you say **runs.** If you're talking about more than one you say **run.**

d. Everybody, what do you say if you're talking about more than one? (Signal.) *Run.*
- What do you say if you're talking about one? (Signal.) *Runs.*
- (Repeat step d until firm.)

e. When you say **we,** are you talking about **one** or **more than one?** (Signal.) *More than one.*
- So do you say **run** or **runs?** (Signal.) *Run.*
- When you say **that dog,** are you talking about **one or more than one?** (Signal.) *One.*
- So do you say **run** or **runs?** (Signal.) *Runs.*

f. When you say **Pam,** are you talking about **one** or **more than one?** (Signal.) *One.*
- So do you say **run** or **runs?** (Signal.) *Runs.*
- When you say **Pam's friends,** are you talking about **one** or **more than one?** (Signal.) *More than one.*
- So do you say **run** or **runs?** (Signal.) *Run.*
- (Repeat step f until firm.)

g. I'll say sentences that have a **blank** in them. Tell me if the word **run** or the word **runs** goes in the blank.

h. Listen. They **blank.** Everybody, what word? (Signal.) *Run.*
- Say the sentence. (Signal.) *They run.*
- Listen. Boys and girls **blank.** Everybody, what word? (Signal.) *Run.*
- Say the sentence. (Signal.) *Boys and girls run.*
- Listen. This woman **blank.** Everybody, what word? (Signal.) *Runs.*
- Say the sentence. (Signal.) *This woman runs.*
- (Repeat step h until firm.)

i. Listen. Two men **blank.** Everybody, what word? (Signal.) *Run.*
- Say the sentence. (Signal.) *Two men run.*
- Listen. She **blank.** Everybody, what word? (Signal.) *Runs.*
- Say the sentence. (Signal.) *She runs.*
- Listen. Her pal **blank.** Everybody, what word? (Signal.) *Runs.*
- Say the sentence. (Signal.) *Her pal runs.*
- Listen. Her pals **blank.** Everybody, what word? (Signal.) *Run.*
- Say the sentence. (Signal.) *Her pals run.*
- (Repeat step i until firm.)

j. Find part A on your worksheet. ✔
- These are the sentences we just did. You'll write **one** or **more than one** after each sentence. You'll write **run** or **runs** in each blank.

k. (Tell the students when they should complete the items in parts A and B.)

l. (After the students complete the items, do a workcheck. For each item: Read the item. Call on a student to answer it. If the answer is wrong, say the correct answer.)

Answer Key: Part A: 1. runs; one **2.** run; more than one **3.** runs; one **4.** run; more than one **5.** runs; one **6.** run; more than one **Part B: 1.** 61 **2.** *Figuring Out the Time of Day* **3.** 77 **4.** *The Chief Listens to Bertha*

Lesson 55

SUBJECT—VERB AGREEMENT

Lesson 55

A. Write **one** or **more than one** after each sentence. Write **hop** or **hops** in each blank.

1. Joan and Barry _____ over logs. _____
2. She _____ over logs. _____
3. His dad and her mom _____ over logs. _____
4. This thin man _____ over logs. _____

B.

1. How many selections are listed for lesson 53? _____
2. What's the page number for the first selection in lesson 53?
   _____
3. What's the page number for the second selection in lesson 53?
   _____
4. What's the title of the second selection? _____
5. What's the title of the third selection? _____

---

a. Find part A on your worksheet. ✔
• I'll read the instructions. Write **one** or **more than one** after each sentence. Write **hop** or **hops** in each blank.
• Some of these sentences talk about **one** thing. Other sentences talk about **more than one thing.** Don't write anything yet.
b. Sentence 1. Joan and Barry **blank** over logs. That sentence is talking about **Joan and Barry. Is Joan and Barry** one or more than one? (Signal.) *More than one.*
• So what word goes in the blank? (Signal.) *Hop.*
c. Sentence 2. She **blank** over logs. What is that sentence talking about? (Signal.) *She.*

• So what word goes in the blank? (Signal.) *Hops.*
d. Sentence 3. His dad and her mom **blank** over logs. What is that sentence talking about? (Signal.) *His dad and her mom.*
• So what word goes in the blank? (Signal.) *Hop.*
e. Sentence 4. This thin man **blank** over logs. What is that sentence talking about? (Signal.) *This thin man.*
• So what word goes in the blank? (Signal.) *Hops.*
f. (Tell the students when they should complete the items in parts A and B.)
g. (After the students complete the items, do a workcheck. For each item: Read the item. Call on a student to answer it. If the answer is wrong, say the correct answer.)

Answer Key: Part A: 1. hop; more than one **2.** hops; one **3.** hop; more than one **4.** hops; one
Part B: 1. 4 **2.** 18 **3.** 20 **4.** *Facts About an Ocean Liner* **5.** *Facts About Ocean Water*

Materials: Each student will need a copy of the worksheet for lesson 56 (blackline master 5) and a copy of textbook B.

SUBJECT—VERB AGREEMENT

> **Lesson 56**
>
> **A.** Write **one** or **more than one** after each sentence. Write **sing** or **sings** in each blank.
>
> 1. His dad _____ well. _____
> 2. His dad and mom _____ well. _____
> 3. Those ten kids _____ well. _____
> 4. Her older brothers _____ well. _____
>
> **B.**
> 1. What's the lesson number for the selection that begins on page 374?
>   _____
> 2. What's the title of the selection that begins on page 374?
>   _____
> 3. What's the lesson number for the selection that begins on page 156?
>   _____
> 4. What's the title of the selection that begins on page 156?

a. Find part A on your worksheet. ✔

• I'll read the instructions. Write **one** or **more than one** after each sentence. Write **sing** or **sings** in each blank.

• Some of these sentences talk about **one** thing. Other sentences talk about **more than one thing.** Don't write anything yet.

b. Sentence 1. His dad **blank** well. That sentence is talking about **his dad.** Is **his dad** one or more than one? (Signal.) *One.*

• So what word goes in the blank? (Signal.) *Sings.*

c. Sentence 2. His dad and mom **blank** well. What is that sentence talking about? (Signal.) *His dad and mom.*

• Is **his dad and mom** one or more than one? (Signal.) *More than one.*

• So what word goes in the blank? (Signal.) *Sing.*

d. (Tell the students when they should complete the items in parts A and B.)

e. (After the students complete the items, do a workcheck. For each item: Read the item. Call on a student to answer it. If the answer is wrong, say the correct answer.)

Answer Key: Part A: 1. sings; one **2.** sing, more than one **3.** sing; more than one **4.** sing; more than one.
Part B: 1. 98 **2.** *Andrew Plays in His First Game* **3.** 68 **4.** *Bertha Has a Great Sense of Smell*

Lesson 57

Materials: Each student will need a copy of the worksheet for lesson 57 (blackline master 6) and a copy of textbook B.

SUBJECT—VERB AGREEMENT

Lesson 57

A. Write **one** or **more than one** after each sentence. Write **talk** or **talks** in each blank.

1. She _____ fast. _____
2. That rabbit _____ fast. _____
3. That rabbit and this skunk _____ fast. _____
4. Six bosses _____ fast. _____

B.

1. How many selections are listed for lesson 91? _____
2. What's the page number for the first selection in lesson 91? _____
3. What's the title of the first selection? _____
4. What's the page number for the second selection in lesson 91? _____

---

a. Find part A on your worksheet. ✔

- I'll read the instructions. Write **one** or **more than one** after each sentence. Write **talk** or **talks** in each blank.
- Some of these sentences are about **one** thing. Other sentences are about **more than one thing.** Don't write anything yet.

b. Sentence 1. She **blank** fast. What is that sentence about? **(Signal.)** *She.*

- Is **she** one or more than one? (Signal.) *One.*
- So what word goes in the blank? (Signal.) *Talks.*

c. (Tell the students when they should complete the items in parts A and B.)

d. (After the students complete the items, do a workcheck. For each item: Read the item. Call on a student to answer it. If the answer is wrong, say the correct answer.)

Answer Key: Part A: 1. talks; one **2.** talks; one **3.** talk; more than one **4.** talk; more than one
Part B: 1. 2 **2.** 317 **3.** *Learning About Checks* **4.** 319

Lesson 58

Materials: Each student will need a copy of the worksheet for lesson 58 (blackline master 6) and a copy of textbook B.

TABLE OF CONTENTS

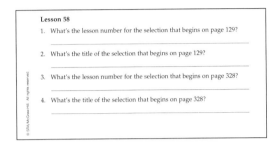

a. (Tell the students when they should complete the items.)

b. (After the students complete the items, do a workcheck. For each item: Read the item. Call on a student to answer it. If the answer is wrong, say the correct answer.)

Answer Key: 1. 65 **2.** *The City of Troy* **3.** 92 **4.** *Andrew Is a Changed Person*

Lesson 59

Materials: Each student will need a copy of the worksheet for lesson 59 (blackline master 7) and a copy of textbook B.

TABLE OF CONTENTS

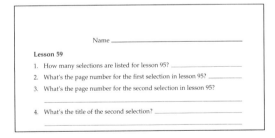

a. (Tell the students when they should complete the items.)

b. (After the students complete the items, do a workcheck. For each item: Read the item. Call on a student to answer it. If the answer is wrong, say the correct answer.)

Answer Key: 1. 2 **2.** 353 **3.** 355 **4.** *The Titans Make Fun of Andrew*

Lesson 60

Materials: Each student will need a copy of the worksheet for lesson 60 (blackline master 7) and a copy of textbook B.

TABLE OF CONTENTS

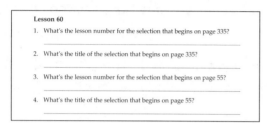

a. (Tell the students when they should complete the items.)

b. (After the students complete the items, do a workcheck. For each item: Read the item. Call on a student to answer it. If the answer is wrong, say the correct answer.)

Answer Key: 1. 93 **2.** *The Strength of Animals* **3.** 57 **4.** *Facts About Coconuts*

Lesson 61

ALPHABETICAL ORDER

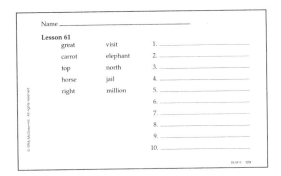

a. You're going to learn about alphabetical order. When you put words in alphabetical order, you look at the first letter of each word. Words that begin with **A** come first. Words that begin with **B** come next. Everybody, what words come after words that begin with **C?** (Signal.) *Words that begin with D.*

• What words come after words that begin with **D?** (Signal.) *Words that begin with E.*

b. Listen. Raise your hand when you know what comes after words that begin with **J.** (Call on a student.) *[Words that begin with K.]*

• Everybody, what comes after words that begin with **J?** (Signal.) *Words that begin with K.*

c. Raise your hand when you know what comes after words that begin with **X.** (Call on a student.) *[Words that begin with Y.]*

• Everybody, what comes after words that begin with **X?** (Signal.) *Words that begin with Y.*

d. Find lesson 61 on your worksheet. ✔

• The words are not in alphabetical order. You'll find the word that should be first in an alphabetical list. No words begin with **A.** So what will you look for next? (Signal.) *Words that begin with B.*

• And if there are no words that begin with **B,** what will you look for next? (Signal.) *Words that begin with C.*

e. Raise your hand when you know which word would be first in an alphabetical list.

• Everybody, which word comes first? (Signal.) *Carrot.*

f. Raise your hand when you know which word comes after **carrot** in the alphabetical list.

• Everybody, which word comes after **carrot?** (Signal.) *Elephant.*

• Yes, there are no words that begin with **D.** But **elephant** begins with **E.**

g. (Write on the board:)

| 1. carrot |
| 2. elephant |

61

- Here are the first two words in the list. Your turn. Copy the first two words in your alphabetical list. Cross out the words **carrot** and **elephant** on your worksheet. That shows that the words are already in your list. Then write the rest of the words in alphabetical order. After you write each word, cross it out on your worksheet. When you're done, all the words should be crossed out. Raise your hand when you're finished. (Observe students and give feedback.)

h. (Write to show:)

1. carrot	6. million
2. elephant	7. north
3. great	8. right
4. horse	9. top
5. jail	10. visit

- Here's what you should have. Fix up any mistakes.
  (Observe students and give feedback.)

Lesson 62

Materials: Each student will need a copy of the worksheet for lesson 62 (blackline master 8).

ALPHABETICAL ORDER

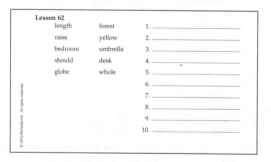

a. Find lesson 62 on your worksheet. ✔
- You're going to put these words in alphabetical order. Figure out which word is the first in the list and write it. Then cross it out on your worksheet. Raise your hand when you're finished. (Observe students and give feedback.)
b. (Write on the board:)

> 1. bedroom

- Here's what you should have for word 1: bedroom.

c. Complete the list. Remember to cross out each word when you write it in your list. (Observe students and give feedback.)
d. (Write to show:)

1. bedroom	6. raise
2. desk	7. should
3. forest	8. umbrella
4. globe	9. whole
5. length	10. yellow

- Check your work. Here's the list you should have. Fix up any mistakes.
  (Observe students and give feedback.)

Lesson 63

Materials: Each student will need a copy of the worksheet for lesson 63 (blackline master 9).

GRAMMAR ELEMENTS

> **Lesson 63**
>
> **A. Write the missing part in each item.**
>
> 1. Jim ran very fast, but Linda ran even _____.
> 2. All of the turtles are slow, but Amy's turtle is the _____.
> 3. Jan said to Al, "Let's go to the store." So Jan and Al _____.
> 4. There was a man in the room. Then another man walked into the room. So now there are two _____.
> 5. When I put my left foot in the tub, I had one wet foot. Then I put my right foot in the tub. So now I have two _____.
> 6. The more you cut a moop's hair, the faster its hair grows. Bob kept cutting his moop's hair, so that moop's hair _____.
>
> **B. Use the words below to make an alphabetical list.**
>
> | only | monkey | 1. _____ |
> | happen | baby | 2. _____ |
> | answer | don't | 3. _____ |
> | zoo | never | 4. _____ |
> | house | perfect | 5. _____ |
> | | | 6. _____ |
> | | | 7. _____ |
> | | | 8. _____ |
> | | | 9. _____ |
> | | | 10. _____ |

a. Find part A on your worksheet. ✔
- I'll read the sentences. You tell me the missing words. Don't write anything.

b. Item 1: Jim ran very fast, but Linda ran even **blank.** Everybody, what word is missing? (Signal.) *Faster.*
- Item 2: All of the turtles are slow, but Amy's turtle is the **blank.** What word is missing? (Signal.) *Slowest.*
- Item 3: Jan said to Al, "Let's go to the store." So Jan and Al **blank.** Everybody, what did they do? (Signal.) *Went to the store.*
- (Repeat step b until firm.)

c. Item 4: There was a man in the room. Then another man walked into the room. So now there are two **blank.** Everybody, what words are missing? (Signal.) *Men in the room.*
- Item 5: When I put my left foot in the tub, I had one wet foot. Then I put my right foot in the tub. So now I have two **blank.** Everybody, what words are missing? (Signal.) *Wet feet.*
- Item 6: The more you cut a moop's hair, the faster its hair grows. Bob kept cutting his moop's hair, so that moop's hair **blank.** What words are missing? (Call on a student. Ideas: *Grew fast, grew faster.*)
- (Repeat step c until firm.)

d. (Tell the students when they should complete the items in parts A and B.)

e. (After the students complete the items, do a workcheck.)
- (For each item in part A: Call on a student to read the sentence saying the words for the blank. If the answer is wrong, say the correct answer.)

Answer Key: Part A: 1. faster **2.** slowest **3.** went to the store **4.** men (in the room) **5.** wet feet **6.** Ideas: grew fast; grew faster
- (For part B, write the alphabetized list on the board:)

1. answer	6. monkey
2. baby	7. never
3. don't	8. only
4. happen	9. perfect
5. house	10. zoo

- Check part B. Here's the list you should have. Fix up any mistakes. ✔

Lesson 64

GRAMMAR ELEMENTS

Lesson 64

A. Write the missing part in each item.

1. Last week Ted lost a tooth. This week the same thing happened. So now Ted has _____.

2. At first one child was in the sandbox. Then another child came into the sandbox. Now there are _____ in the sandbox.

3. We have had some hot days this summer, but today is the _____ day I can remember.

4. Jim said, "I will draw two pictures this week." And that is just what he did. He _____ two pictures.

5. In school, there were three turtles. Ed's turtle was four years old. Greg's turtle was five years old, so it was _____ than Ed's turtle. Bonnie's turtle was 14 years old, so it was the _____ turtle in school.

6. Joe told his mom he would sweep the sidewalk. He started to sweep the sidewalk when his sister asked him, "What are you doing?" Joe said, "I _____."

7. Henry had a loud voice. Tim spoke even _____ than Henry. Ernie spoke the _____ of all.

B. Use the words below to make an alphabetical list.

higher	unless	1. _____
tongue	funny	2. _____
ocean	question	3. _____
yourself	normal	4. _____
insect	knocked	5. _____
		6. _____
		7. _____
		8. _____
		9. _____
		10. _____

---

a. Find part A on your worksheet. ✔

• I'll read the sentences. You tell me the missing words. Don't write anything.

b. Item 1: Last week Ted lost a tooth. This week the same thing happened. So now Ted has **blank.** Everybody, what words are missing? (Signal.) *Two missing teeth.*

• Item 2: At first one child was in the sandbox. Then another child came into the sandbox. Now there are **blank** in the sandbox. What words are missing? (Signal.) *Two children.*

• Item 3: We have had some hot days this summer, but today is the **blank** day I can remember. What word is missing? (Signal.) *Hottest.*

• (Repeat step b until firm.)

c. Item 4: Jim said, "I will draw two pictures this week." And that is just what he did. He **blank** two pictures. Everybody, what word is missing? (Signal.) *Drew.*

• Item 5: In school, there were three turtles. Ed's turtle was four years old. Greg's turtle was five years old, so it was **blank** than Ed's turtle. What word is missing? (Signal.) *Older.*

• Bonnie's turtle was 14 years old, so it was the **blank** turtle in school. What word is missing? (Signal.) *Oldest.*

• (Repeat step c until firm.)

d. Item 6: Joe told his mom he would sweep the sidewalk. He started to sweep the sidewalk when his sister asked him, "What are you doing?" Joe said, "I **blank**." Everybody, what words are missing? (Signal.) *Am sweeping the sidewalk.*

- Item 7: Henry had a loud voice. Tim spoke even **blank** than Henry. What word is missing? (Signal.) *Louder.*
- Ernie spoke the **blank** of all. What word is missing? (Signal.) *Loudest.*
- (Repeat step d until firm.)

e. (Tell the students when they should complete the items in parts A and B.)

f. (After the students complete the items, do a workcheck.)

- (For each item in part A: Call on a student to read the sentence saying the words for the blank. If the answer is wrong, say the correct answer.)

Answer Key: Part A: 1. two missing teeth **2.** two children **3.** hottest **4.** drew **5.** older; oldest **6.** am sweeping (the sidewalk) **7.** louder; loudest

- (For part B, write the alphabetized list on the board:)

1. funny	6. ocean
2. higher	7. question
3. insect	8. tongue
4. knocked	9. unless
5. normal	10. yourself

- Check your work for part B. Here's the list you should have. Fix up any mistakes. ✔

Lesson 65

Materials: Each student will need a copy of the worksheet for lesson 65 (blackline master 12 and lined paper).

EXERCISE 1
TAKING NOTES

a. (Write on the board:)

turtles	petunia
grasshoppers	goose
parrot	redwood tree

- I'm going to read a passage to you. You're going to write a report that retells the same passage.

b. (Write on the board:)

How Long Living Things Live

- Here's the title of the passage you'll write. Copy the title on the first line of your lined paper. ✔
c. When I tell you the facts, you'll write notes. The notes will remind you of the parts that I tell and remind you which part comes first and which parts come next.
d. Listen: Part of what I'll tell is about grasshoppers. When you hear that I'm talking about grasshoppers, you'll write the name **grasshoppers.** When you hear that I'm talking about a parrot, you'll write **parrot.** When you hear that I'm talking about redwood trees, you'll write **redwood trees.**

- Listen: Write the name for the first thing I talk about on the first line under the title. Write the name for the next thing I talk about on the next line.
- Touch the place where you'll write your first note. ✔
e. Listen: Some living things live for more than a hundred years. Some living things live less than a year. I'm going to name something now. Listen. A petunia lives for less than a year. It grows from a seed. It blooms. Then in the fall, it dies. Write the name of the thing I talked about.
(Observe students and give feedback.)
- You should have written a name on the line just under the title. Raise your hand if you did. Everybody, what name? **(Signal.)** *Petunia.*
- Fix it up if you got it wrong.
(Observe students and give feedback.)
f. Next part. An animal that lives for less than one year is a grasshopper. It starts out as something that looks like a worm.

By the middle of summer, it changes into a grasshopper. It dies when the weather turns cold in the fall.
Write your note.
(Observe students and give feedback.)

- You should have written a name on the line just under **petunia.** Everybody, what name? (Signal.) *Grasshopper.*
- Fix it up if you got it wrong.
(Observe students and give feedback.)

g. An animal that lives more than 30 years is a goose. A goose is full grown when it is about two years old. Then it lives a long time as a full-grown goose. Write your note.
(Observe students and give feedback.)

- You should have written a name on the line just under **grasshopper.** Everybody, what name? (Signal.) *Goose.*
- Fix it up if you got it wrong.
(Observe students and give feedback.)

h. A bird that lives even longer than a goose is a parrot. Some parrots live for more than 50 years. Write your note.
(Observe students and give feedback.)

- You should have written a name on the line just under **goose.** Everybody, what name? (Signal.) *Parrot.*
- Fix it up if you got it wrong.
(Observe students and give feedback.)

i. Large turtles that live in the sea often live more than 100 years. They grow to become very large. Some weigh more than 200 pounds. Write your note.
(Observe students and give feedback.)

- You should have written a name on the line just under **parrot.** Everybody, what name? (Signal.) *Turtles.*
- Fix it up if you got it wrong.
(Observe students and give feedback.)

j. Many trees live even longer than the sea turtle. The redwood tree grows bigger and bigger for more than 500 years.
Write your note.
(Observe students and give feedback.)

- You should have written a name on the line just under **turtles.** Everybody, what name? (Signal.) *Redwood tree.*
- Fix it up if you got it wrong.
(Observe students and give feedback.)

k. (Collect papers. Students will use them during the next lesson.)

EXERCISE 2
ALPHABETICAL ORDER

Lesson 65
Use the words below to make an alphabetical list.

shovel	dance	1. _____
kitten	usually	2. _____
officer	lifeboat	3. _____
argued	half	4. _____
vacation	raindrop	5. _____
		6. _____
		7. _____
		8. _____
		9. _____
		10. _____

a. (Tell the students when they should complete the worksheet items.)
b. (After the students complete the items, write the alphabetized list on the board:)

1. argued	6. officer
2. dance	7. raindrop
3. half	8. shovel
4. kitten	9. usually
5. lifeboat	10. vacation

- Check your work. Here's the list you should have. Fix up any mistakes. ✔

Lesson 66

Materials: Each student will need the paper with notes from lesson 66 and a copy of the worksheet for lesson 66 (blackline master 12).

EXERCISE 1
TAKING NOTES

a. (Pass back students' papers with notes.)
- Last time, I read a passage and you took notes. You wrote the name for each part of the passage. This time, you're going to write how long each of those living things lives. If it lives for 60 years, you'll write **60 years** after the name. Everybody, if it lives for one year, what do you write after the name? (Signal.) *1 year.*
- If it lives for less than one year, what do you write after the name? (Signal.) *Less than one year.*

b. Listen and write. I won't stop at the end of each part. So write the number of years after the name as soon as you hear the number of years.
- Listen: Some living things live for more than a hundred years. Some living things live less than a year. I'm going to name something now. Listen. A petunia lives for less than a year. It grows from a seed. It blooms. Then in the fall, it dies.
- Next part. An animal that lives for less than one year is a grasshopper. It starts out as something that looks like a worm. By the middle of summer, it changes into a grasshopper. It dies when the weather turns cold in the fall.
- An animal that lives more than 30 years is a goose. A goose is full grown when it is about two years old. Then it lives a long time as a full-grown goose.
- A bird that lives even longer than a goose is a parrot. Some parrots live for more than 50 years.

- Large turtles that live in the sea often live more than 100 years. They grow to become very large. Some weigh more than 200 pounds.
- Many trees live even longer than the sea turtle. The redwood tree grows bigger and bigger for more than 500 years.

c. Check your answers.
- What did you write after the name **petunia?** (Signal.) *Less than one year.*
- What did you write after the name **grasshopper?** (Signal.) *Less than one year.*
- What did you write after the name **goose?** (Signal.) *More than 30 years.*
- What did you write after the name **parrot?** (Signal.) *More than 50 years.*
- What did you write after the name **turtles?** (Signal.) *More than 100 years.*
- What did you write after the name **redwood tree?** (Signal.) *More than 500 years.*

d. Now you can write an account that is like the one that I read. For each of your notes, write a sentence that names the living thing and tells how long that thing lives.
- Here's the sentence that you'll write for the name **petunia:** A petunia lives for less than one year. Everybody, write that sentence. Then on the next line write the sentence for the second name. (Observe students and give feedback.)
- Write the sentences for the rest of your notes. (Observe students and give feedback.)

e. Let's check your sentences. (Call on individual students to read their sentences. Each sentence should name the living thing and tell how long it lives. Ideas: *A petunia lives for less than one year. A grasshopper lives for less than one year. A goose lives for More than 30 years. A parrot lives for More than 50 years. Turtles live for More than 100 years. Redwood trees live for More than 500 years.*)

EXERCISE 2
ALPHABETICAL ORDER

Lesson 66

Use the words below to make an alphabetical list.

label	unload	1.
enormous	decide	2.
rabbit	peaceful	3.
voice	middle	4.
captain	forever	5.
		6.
		7.
		8.
		9.
		10.

a. (Tell the students when they should complete the worksheet items.)

b. (After the students complete the items, write the alphabetized list on the board:)

1. captain	6. middle
2. decide	7. peaceful
3. enormous	8. rabbit
4. forever	9. unload
5. label	10. voice

• Check your work. Here's the list you should have. Fix up any mistakes. ✔

Lesson 67

EXERCISE 1
OUTLINING

Lesson 67

A.

1. clothing
   A. _____
   B. _____
   C. _____
   D. _____
2. tools
   A. _____
   B. _____
   C. _____
   D. _____
3. vehicles
   A. _____
   B. _____
   C. _____
   D. _____

B.

coat	mirror	1. _____
climb	myna	2. _____
canned	metal	3. _____
curly	money	4. _____
crazy	machine	5. _____

a. Find part A on your worksheet. ✔
• This is an outline. It has three numbers. Touch number 1. ✔
• Everybody, what's the name for number 1? (Signal.) *Clothing.*
• What's name 2? (Signal.) *Tools.*
• What's name 3? (Signal.) *Vehicles.*
b. Under each name, you're going to list four things that are in the class. Each thing will have a letter—A, B, C, or D.
• Name 1 is **clothing.** You could write **socks** after letter **A,** another article of clothing for **B,** another for **C,** and another for **D.** Raise your hand when you're finished.
  (Observe students and give feedback.)
c. (Call on individual students to read each letter and the article of clothing they wrote.)

d. Everybody, touch number 2. What's the name? (Signal.) *Tools.*
• So what are you going to write under **tools?** (Call on a student. Idea: *Names of tools.*)
• Everybody, write a tool for **A,** another for **B,** another for **C,** and another for **D.** Raise your hand when you're finished. (Observe students and give feedback.)
e. (Call on individual students to read each letter and the name of the tool they wrote.)
f. Everybody, touch number 3. What's the name? (Signal.) *Vehicles.*
• So what are you going to write under **vehicles?** (Call on a student. Ideas: *Names of vehicles.*)
• Everybody, write a vehicle for **A,** another for **B,** another for **C,** and another for **D.** Raise your hand when you're finished. (Observe students and give feedback.)
g. (Call on individual students to read each letter and the name of the vehicle they wrote.)
h. Remember how this kind of outline works. You're going to do other outlines later.

EXERCISE 2
ALPHABETICAL ORDER
a. Find part B on your worksheet. ✔
• You've put lists of words in alphabetical order. For each list you've worked with, all the words started with different letters.

Some lists have more than one word that starts with the same letter. What do you do then? You look at the **second** letter in each word.

b. All the words in the star column begin with the letter **C.**

• (Teacher reference:)

coat	curly
climb	crazy
canned	

• Look at the **second** letter of each word. Find the second letter that comes before the others in the alphabet. Raise your hand when you've found the second letter that comes earliest. (Wait.)

• Everybody, which second letter comes earliest? (Signal.) *A.*

• So the word **canned** would come first in an alphabetical list.

• (Write on the board:)

1. canned

c. Raise your hand when you know which second letter comes next in an alphabetical list. (Wait.)

• Everybody, which second letter comes next in the list? (Signal.) *L.*

• So the first two words are **canned** and **climb.**

• (Write to show:)

1. canned
2. climb

d. Raise your hand when you know which second letter comes after **L.**(Wait.)

• Everybody, which second letter comes after **L?** (Signal.) *O.*

• So **coat** is the third word in the list.

• (Write to show:)

2. climb
3. coat

e. Raise your hand when you know which second letter comes after **O.** (Wait.)

• Everybody, which second letter comes after **O.** (Signal.) *R.*

• So which word comes after **coat?** (Signal.) *Crazy.*

• (Write to show:)

3. coat
4. crazy

f. And which second letter comes after **R?** (Signal.) *U.*

• So which word is last in the list? (Signal.) *Curly.*

• (Write to show:)

4. crazy
5. curly

g. Find the moon column on your worksheet. ✔

• All the words in the moon column begin with the letter **M.** Underline the second letter in each word so you'll see the letters you are using. Then write the words in alphabetical order. (Observe students and give feedback.)

h. (Write on the board:)

1. machine	4. money
2. metal	5. myna
3. mirror	

• Check your work. Here's what you should have. Fix up any mistakes. ✔

Lesson 68

Materials: Each student will need a copy of the worksheet for lesson 68 (blackline master 14).

EXERCISE 1
OUTLINING

Lesson 68

A.

1. fruits

⭐ _____

_____

_____

_____

2. vegetables

_____

_____

_____

_____

3. animals

_____

_____

_____

_____

B. Underline the second letter in each word. Then write the words in alphabetical order.

oven   1. _____

once   2. _____

officer   3. _____

ocean   4. _____

outfit   5. _____

a. Find part A on your worksheet. ✔
- This is an outline. It has three numbers. Touch number 1. ✔
- Everybody, what's the name for number 1? (Signal.) *Fruits.*
- What's name 2? (Signal.) *Vegetables.*
- What's name 3? (Signal.) *Animals.*

b. Under each name, you're going to list four things that are in the class. Each thing will have a letter—A, B, C, or D.
- Name 1 is **fruits.** Label the four lines under **fruits** with A, B, C, D. The star shows where you'll write the letter **A.** Raise your hand when you're finished. (Observe students and give feedback.)

- Now write letters for the four lines under **vegetables** and letters for the four lines under **animals.** (Observe students and give feedback.)

c. Your turn to complete your outlines. Write the name of four fruits under **fruits,** four vegetables under **vegetables,** and four animals under **animals.** Raise your hand when you're finished. ✔ (Observe students and give feedback.)

d. (Call on individual students to read the letters and names they wrote for one of the categories.)

e. Remember how this kind of outline works. Next time, you're going to make a complete outline.

EXERCISE 2
ALPHABETICAL ORDER

a. Find part B on your worksheet. ✔
- All the words in part B begin with the letter **O.** Underline the second letter in each word. Then write the words in alphabetical order. (Observe students and give feedback.)

b. (Write on the board:)

1. ocean	4. outfit
2. officer	5. oven
3. once	

- Check your work. Here's what you should have. Fix up any mistakes. ✔

Lesson 69

EXERCISE 1
OUTLINING

Lesson 69

A. containers   games   holidays

_____
_____
_____
_____
_____
_____
_____
_____
_____
_____
_____
_____

B. Underline the second letter in each word. Then write the words in alphabetical order.

swallow	second	1. _____	5. _____
squirrel	solid	2. _____	6. _____
steady	smelly	3. _____	7. _____
scale	shelves	4. _____	8. _____

a. Find part A on your worksheet. ✔
• At the top of the page are three names—containers, games, and holidays. Those are the three main names for your outline. You'll write a number in front of each of those names. Below each name, you'll list four kinds of things.
• The first part of the outline will show containers. Everybody, what number will you write for **containers?** (Signal.) *One.*

• Write the number **1** and the name **containers.** Then write the letters underneath it and write four kinds of containers. Raise your hand when you're finished.
(Observe students and give feedback.)
b. (Call on individual students to read each letter and name of the container they wrote.)
c. The next part of the outline will show games. Everybody, what number will you write for games? (Signal.) *Two.*
• Write the number **2** and the name **games.** Then write the letters underneath it and write four kinds of games. Write the names of four games you play—tag, hide and seek, checkers, baseball, or any other game.
• Then fix up the outline for the last name. That's **holidays.** You'll write the names of four holidays. You can include Halloween, Mother's Day, the Fourth of July, Christmas, New Year's, or any other holiday. Raise your hand when you're finished.
(Observe students and give feedback.)
d. (Call on individual students to read their outline. They are to read each number or letter that precedes a name.)

EXERCISE 2

ALPHABETICAL ORDER

a. Find part B on your worksheet. ✔

- All those words begin with the letter **S.** Underline the second letter in each word. Then write the words in alphabetical order.

  (Observe students and give feedback.)

b. (Write on the board:)

1. scale	5. solid
2. second	6. squirrel
3. shelves	7. steady
4. smelly	8. swallow

- Check your work. Here's what you should have. Fix up any mistakes. ✔

Lesson 70

EXERCISE 1
OUTLINING

Lesson 70

A.   Things I Did

_____day   _____day   _____day

B. All the words in the box begin with the letter **B**. Underline the second letter in each word. Then write the words in alphabetical order.

boast	breath	1. _____	4. _____
building	beyond	2. _____	5. _____
blew	billows	3. _____	6. _____

a. Find part A on your worksheet. ✔
• At the top of the page is the main title, *Things I Did.* You're going to make an outline that shows four things you did on three different days. First write in the names of the days you want to write about. If one of the days you want to write about is Saturday, fix up one of the names that says **blank day** to say **Saturday.** Then fix up the other two names so they tell about the other days you want.
(Observe students and give feedback.)
b. Now write your outline. For the first part of your outline, you'll write a number.

Everybody, what number? (Signal.) *One.*
• Then you'll write **on Saturday,** or **on Sunday,** or **on Tuesday.** Write the title for part one. Then list four things you did on that day. Raise your hand when you've done that much.
(Observe students and give feedback.)
c. (Call on individual students to read the first part of their outline. They are to read each number or letter that precedes the item.)
d. Now complete your outline. Remember to write the numbers and the letters. Raise your hand when you're finished.
(Observe students and give feedback.)
e. (Call on individual students to read their outline.)

EXERCISE 2
ALPHABETICAL ORDER

a. (Tell the students when they should complete the items in part B.)
b. (After the students complete the items, write the alphabetized list on the board:)

1. beyond	4. boast
2. billows	5. breath
3. blew	6. building

• Check your work. Here's the list you should have. Fix up any mistakes. ✔

Lesson 71

Materials: Each student will need a copy of the worksheets for lesson 71 (blackline masters 17 and 18).

EXERCISE 1
FACT VS. OPINION

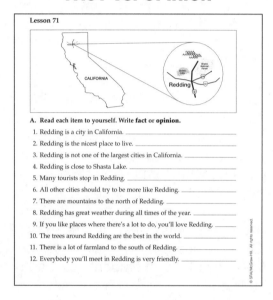

Lesson 71

CALIFORNIA

Redding

A. Read each item to yourself. Write fact or opinion.

1. Redding is a city in California. _____
2. Redding is the nicest place to live. _____
3. Redding is not one of the largest cities in California. _____
4. Redding is close to Shasta Lake. _____
5. Many tourists stop in Redding. _____
6. All other cities should try to be more like Redding. _____
7. There are mountains to the north of Redding. _____
8. Redding has great weather during all times of the year. _____
9. If you like places where there's a lot to do, you'll love Redding. _____
10. The trees around Redding are the best in the world. _____
11. There is a lot of farmland to the south of Redding. _____
12. Everybody you'll meet in Redding is very friendly. _____

B. All the words in the box below begin with the letter E. Underline the second letter in each word. Then write the words in alphabetical order.

eraser	evening
enormous	escape
edge	eggs
easy	eyes

1. _____
2. _____
3. _____
4. _____
5. _____
6. _____
7. _____
8. _____

a. Find part A on your worksheet. ✔
• The map shows Redding, California, and the area around Redding. The population of Redding is about 80 thousand people. That's not one of the larger cities in California. But a lot of tourists stop in Redding because there is a big lake nearby and to the north there are great mountains.

b. All of the statements below the map are about Redding. Some of the statements are true. Those are **facts.** Some of the statements are **opinions.** They are not facts. If you ask different people, you'll get different opinions. Remember, if you can show that something is true, it is a fact. If you can't show it's true, it's an opinion.

c. Statement 1: Redding is a city in California. Everybody, is that a **fact** or is that an **opinion?** (Signal.) *Fact.*

d. Statement 2: Redding is the nicest place to live. Is that a **fact** or is that an **opinion?** (Signal.) *Opinion.*

e. Everybody, work the rest of the items. Read each item to yourself. Write **fact** or **opinion.**

f. (After the students complete the items, do a workcheck. For each item: Read the item. Call on a student to say the answer. If the answer is wrong, say the correct answer.)

Answer Key: 1. fact **2.** opinion **3.** fact **4.** fact **5.** fact **6.** opinion **7.** fact **8.** opinion **9.** opinion **10.** opinion **11.** fact **12.** opinion

EXERCISE 2
ALPHABETICAL ORDER
a. (Tell the students when they should complete the items in part B.)
b. (After the students complete the items, write the alphabetized list on the board:)

1. easy	5. eraser
2. edge	6. escape
3. eggs	7. evening
4. enormous	8. eyes

• Check your work. Here's the list you should have. Fix up any mistakes. ✔

Lesson 72

Materials: Each student will need a copy of the worksheet for lesson 72 (blackline master 19).

ALPHABETICAL ORDER

Lesson 72

A.

change	1. _____
cabbage	2. _____
dollar	3. _____
coast	4. _____
decide	5. _____
dream	6. _____
circus	7. _____

B. Read each item to yourself. Write **fact** or **opinion**.

1. Motorcycling is more fun than anything else. _____
2. Most new motorcycles cost more than $6000. _____
3. Motorcycles get better gas mileage than cars. _____
4. The best looking motorcycles are red. _____
5. Passengers on motorcycles are always comfortable. _____
6. When roads are icy or slippery, motorcycles may be dangerous. _____
7. Everybody who loves speed loves motorcycles. _____

a. Find part A on your worksheet. ✔
• The list of words in the box has words that begin with **C** and words that begin with **D.** Everybody, which comes first in the alphabet, words that begin with **C** or words that begin with **D?** (Signal.) *Words that begin with C.*
b. Circle each word that begins with **C.** Raise your hand when you've done that much. (Observe students and give feedback.)
• The words you should have circled are **change, cabbage, coast,** and **circus.** Fix up any mistakes. ✔
• You'll put all those circled words in your list before you put in any of the words that begin with **D.**
c. Listen: Underline the second letter of each word that begins with **C.** Those are the words you circled.
(Observe students and give feedback.)

d. Now write all the **C** words in alphabetical order. Remember to look at the second letter of each word. Raise your hand when you're finished.
(Observe students and give feedback.)
e. (Write on the board:)

> 1. **cabbage**
> 2. **change**
> 3. **circus**
> 4. **coast**

• Check your work. Here's what you should have so far. Fix up any mistakes. ✔
f. Now you're going to put all the words that begin with **D** in your list. Underline the second letter of each **D** word and write the **D** words in alphabetical order after the **C** words. Raise your hand when you're finished. (Observe students and give feedback.)
g. (Write to show:)

> 4. **coast**
> 5. **decide**
> 6. **dollar**
> 7. **dream**

• Check your work. Here's what you should have. Raise your hand if you got everything right.

EXERCISE 2
FACT VS. OPINION

a. Find part B on your worksheet. ✔

• All of these statements have something to do with motorcycles. Some of the statements are facts. Some of the statements are opinions. Everybody, what do we call a statement that we can show is true? (Signal.) *Fact.*

• What do we call a statement that we **cannot** show is true? (Signal.) *Opinion.*

b. Statement 1: Motorcycling is more fun than anything else. Everybody, is that a **fact** or is that an **opinion?** (Signal.) *Opinion.*

c. Statement 2: Most new motorcycles cost more than $6,000. Everybody, is that a **fact** or is that an **opinion?** (Signal.) *Fact.*

d. (Tell the students when they should complete the items.)

e. (After the students complete the items, do a workcheck. For each item: Read the item. Call on a student to say the answer. If the answer is wrong, say the correct answer.)

Answer Key: 1. opinion **2.** fact **3.** fact **4.** opinion **5.** opinion **6.** fact **7.** opinion

Lesson 73

Materials: Each student will need a copy of the worksheets for lesson 73 (blackline masters 20 and 21) and lined paper.

EXERCISE 1
TOPICS

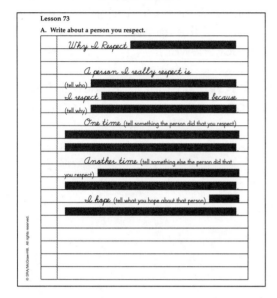

a. Find part A on your worksheet. ✔
- (Write on the board:)

> **respect**

- You're going to write about somebody you really respect. When you respect people, you think they are wise and use good judgement. You know somebody who you really respect.
- You're going to write about that person. Remember, it has to be somebody you know, not the mayor or the President of the United States.

b. Raise your hand if you know who you'd like to write about. ✔
(Call on individual students. Ask:)
- Who do you respect?
- Why do you respect that person? (Praise good reasons.)
- Can you think of one or two things that person does that shows why you respect the person?

c. (Write on the board:)

> **Why I Respect _____**

- Write the title: **Why I Respect** . . . and tell who you respect. (Observe students and give feedback.)

d. (Write on the board:)

> **WHO**

- Start with the words **a person I really respect is** and tell who that person is. Remember to indent. Raise your hand when you're finished. (Observe students and give feedback.)
- (Call on individual students to read their first sentence: *A person I really respect is _____.*)

e. (Write on the board:)

WHY

- Write one or two sentences that tell what you respect about that person. Do you have respect for the person's courage or the person's work, or do you respect the things that the person does? Raise your hand when you've written one or two sentences that tell why you respect the person.
(Observe students and give feedback.)
- (Call on individual students to read their sentences. Praise sentences that clearly specify the reasons.)

f. (Write on the board:)

EXAMPLES

- Now you're going to give two examples of something the person did that you really respect. Start with the words **one time** and tell what happened one time. Remember to indent. Raise your hand when you've written that much.
(Observe students and give feedback.)
- Start the next paragraph with the words **another time** and tell what the person you respect did another time. Raise your hand when you're finished.
(Observe students and give feedback.)
- (Call on individual students to read their examples. Praise good accounts. Offer suggestions for sentences that are vague or that don't provide much detail.)

g. (Write on the board:)

I hope _____.

- Now write your ending. Tell what you hope. Do you hope to be like that person? Do you hope that you'll have the person's courage or strength? What do you hope? Start with the words **I hope** and tell what you hope about that person. Remember to indent.
(Observe students and give feedback.)
- (Call on individual students to read their ending. Praise good accounts.)

h. (Call on individual students to read their entire account. Praise parts that are good, and offer suggestions about organization, missing parts and parts that need work.)

i. (Collect papers. Mark errors in spelling and usage.)

EXERCISE 2

REWRITING

- (After you return the corrected papers, students are to write a final draft and possibly make an illustration for their account.)

EXERCISE 3

LISTENING SKILLS

- Find part B on your worksheet. ✔
- Follow along while I read. Here are rules for good manners when you're listening:
  1. Look at the person who is talking.
  2. Listen to what the person says.
  3. Don't talk to your neighbors or make jokes while the person is talking.
  4. Think about the parts that are good.
  5. Think of what the person could do to make some of the parts better.

  Follow those rules and you'll become a really good listener.

EXERCISE 4

STUDENT QUESTIONS AND FEEDBACK

- I'm going to call on individual students to read their account. I want you to listen carefully and do the following: Write down one or two questions you would like to ask the reader. Maybe you want to know more about where the reader was when the experience took place. Maybe you want to know more about what happened afterwards. Remember, write down one or more good questions.
- Then I want you to be prepared to tell what you think about the account. Tell about a part of it that you thought was interesting. Or tell what you think the reader could do to make the account more interesting.
- (Call on individual students to read their account and other students to comment.)

EXERCISE 5

ALPHABETICAL ORDER

C.

trouble	1. _____
thought	2. _____
ruler	3. _____
tenth	4. _____
rich	5. _____
twice	6. _____
taste	7. _____
rough	8. _____
return	9. _____

a. Find part C on your worksheet. ✔
- The list of words in the box has words that begin with **T** and words that begin with **R.** Everybody, which comes first in the alphabet, words that begin with **T** or words that begin with **R?** (Signal.) *Words that begin with R.*
b. Circle each word in the box that begins with **R.** Raise your hand when you've done that much.
  (Observe students and give feedback.)

- The words you should have circled are **ruler, rich, rough** and **return.** Fix up any mistakes. ✔
- You'll put all those circled words in your list before you put in any of the words that begin with **T.**
c. Listen: Underline the second letter of each word that begins with **R.** Those are the words you circled.
  (Observe students and give feedback.)
d. Now write all the **R** words in alphabetical order. Remember to look at the second letter of each word. Raise your hand when you're finished.
  (Observe students and give feedback.)
e. (Write on the board:)

> 1. **return**
> 2. **rich**
> 3. **rough**
> 4. **ruler**

- Check your work. Here's what you should have so far. Fix up any mistakes. ✔
f. Now you're going to put all the words that begin with **T** in your list. Underline the second letter of each **T** word and write the **T** words in alphabetical order after the **R** words. Raise your hand when you're finished.
  (Observe students and give feedback.)
g. (Write to show:)

> 4. **ruler**
> 5. **taste**
> 6. **tenth**
> 7. **thought**
> 8. **trouble**
> 9. **twice**

- Check your work. Here's what you should have. Raise your hand if you got everything right.

Lesson 74

Materials: Each student will need a copy of the worksheets for lesson 74 (blackline masters 22 and 23) and lined paper.

EXERCISE 1
ALPHABETICAL ORDER

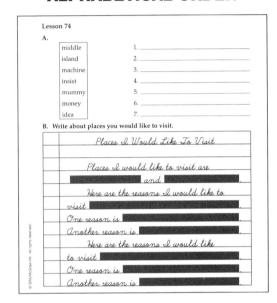

a. **Find part A on your worksheet.** ✔

• The list of words in the box has words that begin with **M** and words that begin with **I.** Everybody, which comes first in the alphabet, words that begin with **M** or words that begin with **I?** (Signal.) *Words that begin with I.*

b. Circle each word in the box that begins with **I.** Raise your hand when you've done that much.
   (Observe students and give feedback.)

• Check your work. The words you should have circled are **island, insist,** and **idea.** Fix up any mistakes.

• You'll put all those circled words in your list before you put in any of the words that begin with **M.**

c. Listen: Underline the second letter of each word that begins with **I.** Those are the words you circled.
   (Observe students and give feedback.)

d. Now write all the **I** words in alphabetical order. Remember to look at the second letter of each word. Raise your hand when you've done that much.
   (Observe students and give feedback.)

e. (Write on the board:)

> 1. idea
> 2. insist
> 3. island

• Check your work. Here's what you should have so far. Fix up any mistakes.

f. Now you're going to put all the words that begin with **M** in your list. Underline the second letter of each **M** word and

write the **M** words in alphabetical order after the **I** words. Raise your hand when you're finished.
(Observe students and give feedback.)
g. (Write to show:)

> 3. **island**
> 4. **machine**
> 5. **middle**
> 6. **money**
> 7. **mummy**

• Check your work. Here's what you should have. Raise your hand if you got everything right.

EXERCISE 2
TOPICS

a. Find part B on your worksheet. ✔
• (Write on the board:)

> **Places I Would Like to Visit**

• You're going to write about a place that you would like to visit. Where would you like to go? Would you like to go some place that you have never been before? Maybe you would like to go someplace familiar to you, a place you have already visited.
• You're going to write about the places you would like to visit. Figure out how many places you're going to tell about. Maybe there is only one place that you really want to visit, or maybe there are two or three places that interest you. Raise your hand if you know one place or two places or three places that interest you. ✔
• (Call on individual students to tell how many places they think they would like to visit and to name those places.)
b. Everybody, write the title to your account. **Places I Would Like to Visit.** Raise your hand when you've written your title.
(Observe students and give feedback.)

c. (Write on the board:)

> **WHICH PLACES**

• Indent and start with the words **I would like to visit** and name the places. Raise your hand when you're finished.
(Observe students and give feedback.)
• (Call on individual students to read their first sentence: *I would like to visit* _____.
d. (Write on the board:)

> **WHY**

• You're going to write a paragraph that tells two reasons why you would like to visit the first place you listed. Start with these words: **Here are the reasons I would like to visit** _____. Write your sentence. Remember to indent. Raise your hand when you've done that much.
(Observe students and give feedback.)
• Now write your reasons. Raise your hand when you've written two reasons you would like to visit the first place you listed. Raise your hand when you're finished.
e. Now you're going to write a paragraph that tells two reasons you would like to visit the second place you listed. Start your paragraph with the words: **Here are the reasons I would like to visit . . .** and name the place. Then give your reasons. Raise your hand when you're finished.
(Observe students and give feedback.)
f. (Repeat step e for directing students to write about other places students had selected.)
g. (Call on individual students to read their entire account. Praise parts that are good, and offer suggestions about organization, missing parts and parts that need work.)
h. (Collect papers. Mark errors in spelling and usage.)

EXERCISE 3

REWRITING

- (After you return the corrected papers, students are to write a final draft and possibly make an illustration for their account.)

EXERCISE 4

LISTENING SKILLS

- Find part C on your worksheet. ✔
- Follow along while I read. Here are rules for good manners when you're listening:
  1. Look at the person who is talking.
  2. Listen to what the person says.
  3. Don't talk to your neighbors or make jokes while the person is talking.
  4. Think about the parts that are good.
  5. Think of what the person could do to make some of the parts better.

  Follow those rules and you'll become a really good listener.

EXERCISE 5

STUDENT QUESTIONS AND FEEDBACK

- I'm going to call on individual students to read their account. I want you to listen carefully and do the following. Write down one or two questions you would like to ask the reader. Maybe you want to know more about where the reader was when the experience took place. Maybe you want to know more about what happened afterwards. Remember, write down one or more good questions.
- Then I want you to be prepared to tell what you think about the account. Tell about a part of it that you thought was interesting. Or tell what you think the reader could do to make the account more interesting.

Lesson 75

Materials: Each student will need a copy of the worksheet for lesson 75 (blackline master 24) and lined paper.

EXERCISE 1
ALPHABETICAL ORDER

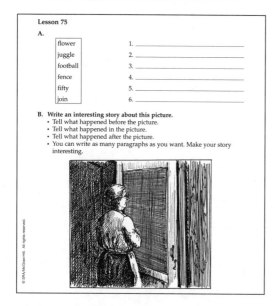

a. Find part A on your worksheet. ✔
- The list of words in the box has words that begin with **J** and words that begin with **F.** Everybody, which comes first in the alphabet, words that begin with **J** or words that begin with **F?** (Signal.) *Words that begin with F.*

b. Circle all the words that begin with **F** and put them in alphabetical order. Then put all the words that begin with **J** in your list. Put those words in alphabetical order.

(Observe students and give feedback.)

c. (Write on the board:)

1. fence	4. football
2. fifty	5. join
3. flower	6. juggle

- Check your work. Here's what you should have. Raise your hand if you got everything right.

EXERCISE 2

PASSAGE WRITING
Vague Picture

a. Find part B on your worksheet. ✔
- You're going to write an interesting story about the picture. You'll tell about what happened **before** the picture, what happened **in** the picture and what happened **after** the picture.
- Remember, first tell what happened before the picture. What do you tell first? (Signal.) *What happened before the picture.*
- What do you tell next? (Signal.) *What happened in the picture.*
- Yes, what happened in the picture. You'll tell what the woman was thinking, feeling and doing.
- What will you tell last? (Signal.) *What happened after the picture.*

b. You can write as many paragraphs as you want. Make your story interesting. Raise your hand when you're finished. (Observe students and give feedback.)

- (Students may do their writing and rewriting on a computer, using word-processing software.)

c. (Call on individual students to read their entire passage. Praise good parts. Offer suggestions about organization, missing parts or parts that need work.)

d. (Collect papers. Mark errors in spelling and usage.)

REWRITING

- (After you return the corrected papers, students are to write a final draft and possibly make an illustration for their account.)

Lesson 76

EXERCISE 1

ALPHABETICAL ORDER

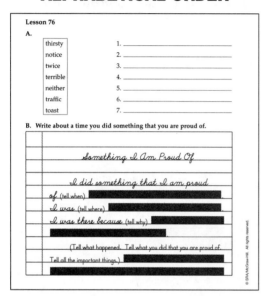

a. Find part A on your worksheet. ✔
• The list of words in the box has words that begin with **N** and words that begin with **T.** Everybody, which comes first in the alphabet, words that begin with **N** or words that begin with **T?** (Signal.) *Words that begin with N.*
b. Circle all the words that begin with **N** and put them in alphabetical order. Then put all the words that begin with **T** in your list. Put those words in alphabetical order.
(Observe students and give feedback.)

c. (Write on the board:)

> 1. neither
> 2. notice
> 3. terrible
> 4. thirsty
> 5. toast
> 6. traffic
> 7. twice

• Check your work. Here's what you should have. Raise your hand if you got everything right.

EXERCISE 2

TOPICS

a. Find part B on your worksheet. ✔
• You're going to write about a time you did something that you were very proud of. First we'll talk about it.
b. (Write on the board:)

> **WHEN**

• Listen: The first thing you'll tell about is when it happened. Was it in the summer or was it in the middle of winter? Do you remember the year it was? Do you remember how old you were?
• Start with the words **I did something that I am proud of** and tell when it happened. (Call on individual students. Praise students who start with the words *I did something that I am proud of* and who give some indication of when.) (To correct: If students start to tell more than **when,** stop them and remind them that they are just telling **when.**)
c. (Write on the board:)

> **WHERE**

- The next thing you'll tell is where it happened. Were you at home or somewhere else? Were you in a car or a house, or were you on your bike? Where were you?
- Start with the words **I was** and tell where you were. You can also tell who you were with. **(Call on individual students. Praise accounts that start with the words** *I was* **and that tell where the student was and possibly who was with the student.)**

d. (Write on the board:)

WHY

- Listen: After you tell about where you were, tell **why** you were there. What were you doing? What did you plan to do?
- Start with the words **I was there because** and tell why you were there. **(Call on individual students. Praise students who start with the words** *I was there because* **and who tell the reason.)** **(To correct: If students tell more than why they were there, stop them and remind them that they are simply telling why they were there.)**

e. (Write on the board:)

WHAT HAPPENED

- After you tell why you were at the place, tell what happened. Tell what you did that you are proud of. Tell all the important things that went on. Tell what you did that you're proud of and why you were proud of what you did. If you helped somebody else, tell how that person felt and what that person said. **(Call on individual students. Praise accounts that give details about what happened.)**

f. (Write on the board:)

Something I Am Proud of

- Now you're going to write your report on lined paper. Copy the title on the top line of your paper. Raise your hand when you've done that much.
  (Observe students and give feedback.)

g. First you'll tell when. Start with the words **I did something that I am proud of** and tell when it happened. Write one or more sentences. Remember to indent. Raise your hand when you've done that much.
  (Observe students and give feedback.)

h. Now you're going to tell where you were. Start with the words **I was** and tell where you were. If you were with somebody else, you can also tell who was with you. Raise your hand when you've written about where you were.
  (Observe students and give feedback.)

i. Now you're going to tell why you were there. Start with the words **I was there because** and tell why you were there. Tell what you planned to do there. Raise your hand when you're finished.
  (Observe students and give feedback.)

j. Now you're going to write about what you did that you are proud of. Remember, tell what you did that you are proud of and tell why you are proud of it. Tell how you felt. If you helped somebody else, tell what that person said. Raise your hand when you're finished.
  (Observe students and give feedback.)

- Now you can write an ending. You can tell what happened later on. Raise your hand when you're finished.
  (Observe students and give feedback.)

k. I'm going to call on individual students to read their account. I want you to listen carefully and do the following. Write down one or two questions you would like to ask the reader. Maybe you want to know more about where the reader was when the experience took place. Maybe you want to know more about what happened afterwards. Remember, write down one or more good questions.

- Then I want you to be prepared to tell what you think about the account. Tell about a part of it that you thought was interesting. Or tell what you think the reader could do to make the account more interesting.
- (Call individual students to read their account and other students to comment.)

l. (Collect papers and give feedback for changes. Mark sentences that do not have ending marks. Mark parts that do not tell what they are supposed to tell.)

REWRITING

- (Students are later to revise their papers and incorporate the changes you indicated.)
- (After revising their reports, have them illustrate their reports with a picture that shows them doing something they are proud of. They may write labels for the people or things in the picture.)

EXERCISE 1

PASSAGE WRITING
Vague Picture

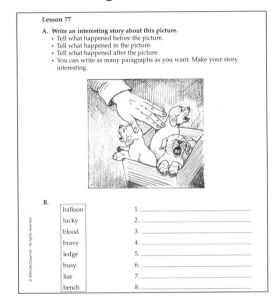

a. Find part A on your worksheet. ✔
• You're going to write an interesting story about the picture. You'll tell about what happened before the picture, what happened in the picture and what happened after the picture.
• Remember, first tell what happened before the picture. What do you tell first? (Signal.) *What happened before the picture.*
• What do you tell next? (Signal.) *What happened in the picture.*
  Yes, what happened in the picture. You'll tell what the puppies were thinking, feeling and doing. Tell about the person whose hand is shown.
• What will you tell last? (Signal.) *What happened after the picture.*
b. You can write as many paragraphs as you want. Make your story interesting. Raise your hand when you're finished. (Observe students and give feedback.)

• (Students may do their writing and rewriting on a computer.)
c. (Call on individual students to read their entire passage. Praise good parts. Offer suggestions about organization, missing parts or parts that need work.)
d. (Collect papers. Mark mistakes in spelling and usage.)

EXERCISE 2

REWRITING
• (After you return the corrected papers, students are to write a final draft and possibly illustrate their account.)

EXERCISE 3

ALPHABETICAL ORDER
a. Find part B on your worksheet. ✔
• The list of words in the box has words that begin with **L** and words that begin with **B.** Everybody, which comes first in the alphabet, words that begin with **L** or words that begin with **B?** (Signal.) *Words that begin with B.*
b. Circle all the words that begin with **B** and put them in alphabetical order. Then put all the words that begin with **L** in your list. Put those words in alphabetical order. (Observe students and give feedback.)
c. (Write on the board:)

1. balloon	5. busy
2. bench	6. ledge
3. blood	7. liar
4. brave	8. lucky

• Check your work. Here's what you should have. Raise your hand if you got everything right.

Lesson 78

EXERCISE 1
ALPHABETICAL ORDER

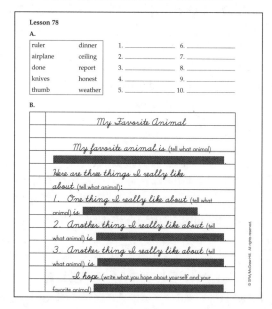

a. Find part A on your worksheet. ✔

• Here's a list of words that you'll put in alphabetical order. Most of the words do not begin with the same letter, but two words begin with **D** and two words begin with **R.**

b. First write the words that come before **D.** Don't write **done** or **dinner,** but write all the words that come before **done** or **dinner.**
(Observe students and give feedback.)

c. (Write on the board:)

> **1. airplane**
> **2. ceiling**

• Check your work. Here are the words you should have so far. Fix up any mistakes.

d. Now put **done** and **dinner** in the list. Look at the second letter of each word to see which word comes first and which word comes next.
(Observe students and give feedback.)

e. (Write to show:)

> **2. ceiling**
> **3. dinner**
> **4. done**

• Check your work. Here's what you should have. Fix up any mistakes.

f. Now write the words that come after **D** but before **R.** Don't write the words that begin with **R.**
(Observe students and give feedback.)

g. (Write to show:)

> **4. done**
> **5. honest**
> **6. knives**

• Check your work. Here's what you should have. Fix up any mistakes.

h. Now put in the words that begin with **R.** Remember, look at the second letters. Then write the rest of the words in the list.
(Observe students and give feedback.)

i. (Write to show:)

> **6. knives**
> **7. report**
> **8. ruler**
> **9. thumb**
> **10. weather**

- Check your work. Here's what you should have. Raise your hand if you got everything right.

EXERCISE 2
TOPICS

a. Find part B on your worksheet. ✔
- (Write on the board:)

> **My Favorite Animal**

- You're going to write about your favorite animal and tell why you like that animal.
- Raise your hand if you know what you'd like to write about. ✔
  (Call on individual students. Ask: What are you going to write about?)

b. The title is: **My Favorite Animal.** Write the title.
  (Observe students and give feedback.)

c. (Write on the board:)

> **What Animal**

- Write a sentence that names your favorite animal. Raise your hand when you're finished.
  (Observe students and give feedback.)
- (Call on individual students to read their first sentence.)

d. (Write on the board:)

> **WHY**
> 1.
> 2.
> 3.

- You're going to make a list of three things you like about the animal. Start with the words **here are three things I really like about** . . . and name the animal. Raise your hand when you've written that sentence.
  (Observe students and give feedback.)
- (Call on individual students to read their sentence.)

e. On the next line write the number 1 and a period. Then write a sentence that tells one thing you like. Maybe you like horses because you can ride them. Or maybe you like dogs because they are always happy to be around you. Start with the words **one thing I really like about.** Raise your hand when you've written your sentence for number 1. Remember, just tell about one thing you like.
  (Observe students and give feedback.)
- (Call on students to read what they've written for number 1.)

f. Now write the number 2 and a period on the next line. On that line, write your sentence for number 2. Raise your hand when you're finished.
  (Observe students and give feedback.)
- (Call on students to read their sentence for number 2.)

g. Now write the number 3 and a period on the next line. On that line, write your sentence for number 3. Raise your hand when you're finished.
  (Observe students and give feedback.)
- (Call on students to read their sentence for number 3.)

h. (Write on the board:)

> **I hope _____.**

- Now write your ending. Tell what you hope. Do you hope that you'll get a dog for your birthday? Do you hope that you can go horseback riding sometime? Write what you hope. Raise your hand when you're finished.
  (Observe students and give feedback.)

i. I'm going to call on individual students to read their account. I want you to listen carefully and do the following. Write down one or two questions you would like to ask the reader. Maybe you want to know more about where the reader was when the experience took place. Maybe you want to know more about what happened afterwards. Remember, write down one or more good questions.

• Then I want you to be prepared to tell what you think about the account. Tell about a part of it that you thought was interesting. Or tell what you think the reader could do to make the account more interesting.

• (Call individual students to read their account and other students to comment.)

j. (Collect papers. Mark mistakes in spelling and usage.)

EXERCISE 3
REWRITING

• (After you return the corrected papers, students are to write a final draft and possibly make an illustration for their account.)

Lesson **79**

Materials: Each student will need a copy of the worksheet for lesson 79 (blackline master 28), lined paper, and illustrating materials.

EXERCISE 1
ALPHABETICAL ORDER

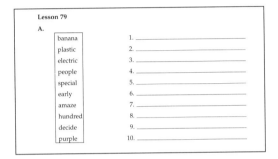

```
Lesson 79
A.
   banana        1. _____
   plastic       2. _____
   electric      3. _____
   people        4. _____
   special       5. _____
   early         6. _____
   amaze         7. _____
   hundred       8. _____
   decide        9. _____
   purple       10. _____
```

a. Find lesson 79 on your worksheet. ✔

• Here's a list of words that you'll put in alphabetical order. Most of the words do not begin with the same letter, but two words begin with **E** and three words begin with **P**.

b. First write the words that come before **E**. Don't write **electric** or **early,** but write all the words that come before **electric** or **early.**
   (Observe students and give feedback.)

c. (Write on the board:)

> **1. amaze**
> **2. banana**
> **3. decide**

•Check your work. Here are the words you should have so far. Fix up any mistakes.

d. Now put **electric** and **early** in the list. Look at the second letter of each word to see which word comes first and which word comes next.
   (Observe students and give feedback.)

e. (Write to show:)

> **3. decide**
> **4. early**
> **5. electric**

• Check your work. Here's what you should have. Fix up any mistakes.

f. Now write the words that come after **E** but before **P.** Don't write the words that begin with **P.**
   (Observe students and give feedback.)

g. (Write to show:)

> **4. early**
> **5. electric**
> **6. hundred**

• Check your work. Here's what you should have. Fix up any mistakes.

h. Now put in the words that begin with **P.** Remember, look at the second letters. Then write the rest of the words in the list.
   (Observe students and give feedback.)

i. (Write to show:)

> 6. hundred
> 7. people
> 8. plastic
> 9. purple
> 10. special

- Check your work. Here's what you should have. Raise your hand if you got everything right.

EXERCISE 2
TOPICS

a. You're going to write about something that was very easy for you to do. Maybe it was something in school that you had no trouble learning or doing. Maybe it was something like learning to ride a bike, or learning to skateboard.
b. First we'll talk about it.
- (Write on the board:)

WHEN

- Listen: The first thing you'll tell about is **when** it happened. Do you remember the year it was? Do you remember how old you were?
- Start with the words **I did something that was really easy for me to do** and tell when it happened. (Call on individual students. Praise students who start with the words *I did something really easy for me to do* and who give some indication of when.)
(To correct: If students start to tell more than **when,** stop them and remind them that they are just telling **when.**)
c. (Write on the board:)

WHERE

- The next thing you'll tell is where it happened. Start with the words **I was** and tell where you were. You can also tell who you were with. (Call on individual students. Praise accounts that start with the words **I was** and that tell where the student was and possibly who was with the student.)
d. (Write on the board:)

WHAT

- The next thing you'll tell is what was really easy for you to do. (Call on individual students. Praise accounts that tell what was easy for the students.)
e. (Write on the board:)

WHAT HAPPENED

- Now you'll tell what happened. Tell all the important things that went on. Tell why it was important for you to do it. Tell how you did it and how you felt. (Call on individual students. Praise accounts that give details about what happened.)
f. (Write on the board:)

Something That Was Easy for Me

- Now you're going to write your report on lined paper. Copy the title on the top line of your paper. Raise your hand when you've done that much.
(Observe students and give feedback.)
g. Now you'll tell when. Start with the words **I did something that was easy for me to do** and tell when it happened. Write one or more sentences. Remember to indent your first sentence. Raise your hand when you've written about when it happened.
(Observe students and give feedback.)
h. Now you're going to tell where you were. Start with the words **I was** and tell where you were. If you were with somebody else, you can also tell that they were with you. Raise your hand when you've written about where you were.
(Observe students and give feedback.)

i. Now you're going to tell what happened. Remember, tell about what was easy for you and why you think it was so easy for you. Raise your hand when you're finished.
(Observe students and give feedback.)

j. Now you can write an ending. You can tell what happened later on. Raise your hand when you're finished.
(Observe students and give feedback.)

k. (Call on individual students to read their entire account. Give feedback about good parts and parts that have problems.)

l. (Collect papers and give feedback for changes. Mark sentences that do not have ending marks. Mark parts that do not tell what they are supposed to tell.)

EXERCISE 3
REWRITING

- (Students are later to revise their papers and incorporate the changes you indicated.)
- (After revising their reports, have them illustrate their reports with a picture that shows them doing what had been easy for them. They may write labels for the people or things in the picture.)

Lesson 80

Materials: Each student will need a copy of the worksheet for lesson 80 (blackline master 29) and lined paper.

EXERCISE 1
ALPHABETICAL ORDER

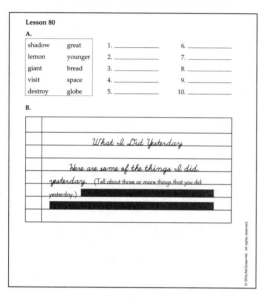

a. Find part A on your worksheet. ✔

• Here's a list of words that you'll put in alphabetical order. Most of the words do not begin with the same letter, but three words begin with **G** and two words begin with **S.**

b. First write the words that come before **G.** Don't write the **G** words, but write all the words that come before the **G** words.

(Observe students and give feedback.)

c. (Write on the board:)

> 1. bread
> 2. destroy

• Check your work. Here are the words you should have so far. Fix up any mistakes.

d. Now put the **G** words in the list. Look at the second letter of each word to see which word comes first.

(Observe students and give feedback.)

e. (Write to show:)

> 2. destroy
> 3. giant
> 4. globe
> 5. great

• Check your work. Here's what you should have. Fix up any mistakes.

f. Now write the words that come after **G** but before **S.** Don't write the words that begin with **S.**

(Observe students and give feedback.)

g. (Write to show:)

> 4. globe
> 5. great
> 6. lemon

• Check your work. Here's what you should have. Fix up any mistakes.

h. Now put in the words that begin with **S.** Remember, look at the second letters. Then write the rest of the words in the list.

(Observe students and give feedback.)

i. (Write to show:)

> 6. lemon
> 7. shadow
> 8. space
> 9. visit
> 10. younger

- Check your work. Here's what you should have. Raise your hand if you got everything right.

EXERCISE 2
TOPICS

a. Find part B on your worksheet. ✔
- (Write on the board:)

What I Did Yesterday

- You're going to write about what you did yesterday.
  (Observe students and give feedback.)
b. You'll write a paragraph that tells what you did yesterday. Begin with a sentence that says: **Here are some of the things I did yesterday.** Then list three or more things that you did yesterday. Maybe you went to school, maybe you watched a little television, or maybe you worked on your homework. Write at least three sentences that tell what you did yesterday. Raise your hand when you're finished.
  (Observe students and give feedback.)
- (Call on individual students to read their sentences. Praise paragraphs that tell about two or three things that the student did yesterday.)

c. I'm going to call on individual students to read their account. I want you to listen carefully and do the following. Write down one or two questions you would like to ask the reader. Maybe you want to know more about where the reader was when the experience took place. Maybe you want to know more about what happened afterwards. Remember, write down one or more good questions.
- Then I want you to be prepared to tell what you think about the account. Tell about a part of it that you thought was interesting. Or tell what you think the reader could do to make the account more interesting.
- (Call individual students to read their account and other students to comment.)
d. (Collect papers. Mark mistakes in spelling and usage.)

EXERCISE 3
REWRITING

- (After you return the corrected papers, students are to write a final draft and possibly make an illustration for their account.)

Lesson 81

Materials: Each student will need a copy of the worksheet for lesson 81 (blackline master 30) and lined paper.

EXERCISE 1

ALPHABETICAL ORDER

a. Find part A on your worksheet. ✔
- (Teacher reference:)

count	cod
collar	coat
complete	cone
cob	cook

- In all the words in the box, the first two letters are the same. All the words begin with the letters **C-O.** To put these words in alphabetical order, you have to look at the **third** letter in the words.
b. Underline the third letter in each word. Raise your hand when you've done that much.
(Observe students and give feedback.)

c. Raise your hand when you know which of these words comes first in the alphabet. (Wait.)
- Everybody, which word comes first? (Signal.) *Coat.*
- Yes, **C-O-A** comes before **C-O-B** or any of the other words that start with **C-O.**
d. Write the words in alphabetical order. Raise your hand when you're finished. **(Observe students and give feedback.)**
e. (Write on the board:)

> 1. coat
> 2. cob
> 3. cod
> 4. collar
> 5. complete
> 6. cone
> 7. cook
> 8. count

- Check your work. Here's what you should have. Fix up any mistakes.

EXERCISE 2

PASSAGE WRITING

VAGUE PICTURE

a. Find part B on your worksheet. ✔
- You're going to write an interesting story about the picture. You'll tell about what happened before the picture, what happened in the picture and what happened after the picture.
- Remember, first tell what happened before the picture. What do you tell first? (Signal.) *What happened before the picture.*

- What do you tell next? (Signal.) *What happened in the picture.*
  Yes, what happened in the picture. You'll tell what the small girl was thinking, feeling and doing.
- What will you tell last? (Signal.) *What happened after the picture.*

b. You can write as many paragraphs as you want. Make your story interesting. Raise your hand when you're finished.
(Observe students and give feedback.)

- (Students may do their writing and rewriting on a computer, using word-processing software.)

c. (Call on individual students to read their entire passage. Praise good parts. Offer suggestions about organization, missing parts or parts that need work.)

d. (Collect papers. Mark mistakes in spelling and usage.)

EXERCISE 3
REWRITING

- (After you return the corrected papers, students are to write a final draft and possibly make an illustration for their account.)

Lesson 82

EXERCISE 1
ALPHABETICAL ORDER

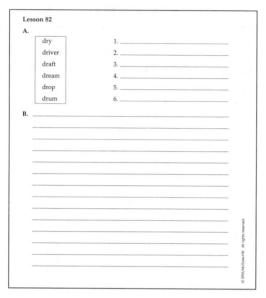

a. Find part A on your worksheet. ✔
- (Teacher reference:)

dry	dream
driver	drop
draft	drum

- All the words in the box begin with the same letters—**D-R.** So you have to look at the third letter of each word to figure out the alphabetical order.
b. Look at the third letter in each word. Then write the words in alphabetical order. Raise your hand when you're finished.
  (Observe students and give feedback.)
c. (Write on the board:)

1. draft	4. drop
2. dream	5. drum
3. driver	6. dry

- Check your work. Here's what you should have. Fix up any mistakes.

EXERCISE 2
TOPICS

a. Find part B on your worksheet. ✔
- You're going to write about a time you helped somebody.
b. (Write on the board:)

WHEN

- Listen: The first thing you'll tell about is when it happened.
- Start with the words **I helped somebody** and tell when it happened. Raise your hand when you've completed your first sentence.
  (Observe students and give feedback.)
- (Call on individual students to read their sentence. Praise students who start with the words *I helped somebody* and who give some indication of when.)
c. (Write on the board:)

WHERE

- The next sentence you'll write tells where it happened. Were you at home or somewhere else? Were you in a car or a house, or were you on your bike? Where were you when you helped somebody?
- Start with the words **I was** and tell where you were. You can also tell who you were with. Raise your hand when you've written the sentence.
  (Observe students and give feedback.)

- (Call on individual students to read their sentence. Praise sentences that start with the words *I was* and that tell where the student was and possibly who was with the student.)
d. (Write on the board:)

WHO
WHY

- Write a sentence that tells who needed help and why that person needed help. Start with the name of the person and tell why the person needed help. Tell the problem the person had. Raise your hand when you're finished.
  (Observe students and give feedback.)
- (Call on individual students to read their sentence. Praise sentences that start with the person's name and tell the problem the person had.)
e. (Write on the board:)

WHAT HAPPENED

- Tell what you did to help the person. Tell all the important things that happened. Raise your hand when you've finished telling about what happened.
  (Observe students and give feedback.)
- (Call on individual students to read their account. Praise accounts that give details about what happened.)
f. (Write on the board:)

LATER

- Now write the last part of your story. Tell what happened later on. Did the person thank you? Was the person grateful because of what you did? Are you glad that you did what you did?
- Start with the words **later on** and tell what happened later on or how you felt later on. You may need more than one sentence to tell this part. Raise your hand when you're finished.
  (Observe students and give feedback.)

- (Call on individual students to read their account.)
g. (Write on the board:)

Proud of Myself

- Copy the title on the top line of your paper. Raise your hand when you're finished.
  (Observe students and give feedback.)
h. I'm going to call on individual students to read their account. I want you to listen carefully and do the following. Write down one or two questions you would like to ask the reader. Maybe you want to know more about where the reader was when the experience took place. Maybe you want to know more about what happened afterwards. Remember, write down one or more good questions.
- Then I want you to be prepared to tell what you think about the account. Tell about a part of it that you thought was interesting. Or tell what you think the reader could do to make the account more interesting.
- (Call individual students to read their account and other students to comment.)
i. (Collect papers and give feedback for changes. Mark sentences that do not have ending marks. Mark parts that do not tell what they are supposed to tell.)

EXERCISE 3
REWRITING

- (Students are later to revise their papers and incorporate the changes you indicated.)
- (After students revise their reports, direct students to illustrate their reports with a picture that shows what happened. They may write labels for the people or things in the picture.)

Lesson 83

Materials: Each student will need a copy of the worksheet for lesson 83 (blackline master 32) and lined paper.

EXERCISE 1
AFFIXES

Lesson 83

A. Some word parts are called prefixes. Prefixes are the first part of some words. Some prefixes have a clear meaning.

Words	Opposites
1. agree	_____
2. appear	_____
3. like	_____
4. join	_____

B. Write an interesting story about this picture.
- Tell what happened before the picture.
- Tell what happened in the picture.
- Tell what happened after the picture.
- You can write as many paragraphs as you want. Make your story interesting.

- I'll read what it says. Follow along. **Some word parts are called prefixes. Prefixes are the first part of some words. Some prefixes have a clear meaning.**
- Everybody, what do we call these word parts? (Signal.) *Prefixes.*
- Do prefixes come at the **beginning** of some words or at the **end** of these words? (Signal.) *At the beginning.*
- And some prefixes have a clear meaning.

b. (Write on the board:)

> **dis**

- The prefix **dis** often means **the opposite of.** What does the prefix **dis** often mean? (Signal.) *The opposite of.*

- So the word **disbelief** means the opposite of the word **belief.** What word means the opposite of **belief?** (Signal.) *Disbelief.*

c. Look at the list of words on your worksheet. ✔
- You're going to tell me the words that mean the opposite of these words.
- Everybody, what's word 1? (Signal.) *Agree.*
- What word means **the opposite of agree?** (Signal.) *Disagree.*
- What's word 2? (Signal.) *Appear.*
- What word means **the opposite of appear?** (Signal.) *Disappear.*
- What's word 3? (Signal.) *Like.*
- What word means **the opposite of like?** (Signal.) *Dislike.*
- Everybody, what's word 4? (Signal.) *Join.*
- What word means **the opposite of join?** (Signal.) *Disjoin.*

d. Write the opposite of each word for lesson 83 using the prefix **dis.** Raise your hand when you're done. **(Observe students and give feedback.)**

e. Check your work. Word 1. What word means **the opposite of agree?** (Signal.) *Disagree.*
- Word 2. What word means **the opposite of appear?** (Signal.) *Disappear.*
- Word 3. What word means **the opposite of like?** (Signal.) *Dislike.*
- Word 4. What word means **the opposite of join?** (Signal.) *Disjoin.*

56 Lesson 83

EXERCISE 2
PASSAGE WRITING

VAGUE PICTURE

a. Find part B on your worksheet. ✔
- You're going to write an interesting story about the picture. You'll tell about what happened before the picture, what happened in the picture and what happened after the picture.
- Remember, first tell what happened before the picture. What do you tell first? (Signal.) *What happened before the picture.*
- What do you tell next? (Signal.) *What happened in the picture.*
  Yes, what happened in the picture. You'll tell what the older man was thinking, feeling and doing.
- What will you tell last? (Signal.) *What happened after the picture.*

b. You can write as many paragraphs as you want. Make your story interesting. Raise your hand when you're finished. (Observe students and give feedback.)
- (Students may do their writing and rewriting on a computer, using word-processing software.)
c. (Call on individual students to read their entire passage. Praise good parts. Offer suggestions about organization, missing parts or parts that need work.)
d. (Collect papers. Mark mistakes in spelling and usage.)

EXERCISE 3
REWRITING

- (After you return the corrected papers, students are to write a final draft and possibly make an illustration for their account.)

Lesson 84

EXERCISE 1
AFFIXES

Lesson 84

A.
1. arrange _____
2. join _____
3. appear _____
4. charge _____

B.
_____
_____
_____
_____
_____
_____
_____
_____
_____
_____
_____
_____
_____
_____

a. You learned a prefix that means **the opposite of.** Everybody, what's that prefix? (Signal.) *Dis.*
• What word means **the opposite of appear?** (Signal.) *Disappear.*
• What word means **the opposite of order?** (Signal.) *Disorder.*
• What word means **the opposite of approve?** (Signal.) *Disapprove.*
b. (Write on the board:)

> **re**

• You're going to write words that have the prefix spelled R-E. The prefix **re** means **again** in some words. Everybody, what does the prefix **re** mean? (Signal.) *Again.*
c. The word **reorder** means **to order again.**

• What does **reorder** mean? (Signal.) *To order again.*
• What does **refill** mean? (Signal.) *To fill again.*
• What does the word **replay** mean? (Signal.) *To play again.*
• (Repeat until firm.)
d. Find part A on your worksheet. ✔
• Everybody, what's word 1? (Signal.) *Arrange.*
• What word means **arrange again?** (Signal.) *Rearrange.*
• What's word 2? (Signal.) *Join.*
• What word means **join again?** (Signal.) *Rejoin.*
• What's word 3? (Signal.) *Appear.*
• What word means **appear again?** (Signal.) *Reappear.*
• What's word 4? (Signal.) *Charge.*
• What word means **charge again?** (Signal.) *Recharge.*
e. Go back to word 1. ✔
• Everybody, what's word 1? (Signal.) *Arrange.*
• What word means **the opposite of arrange?** (Signal.) *Disarrange.*
• What's word 2? (Signal.) *Join.*
• What word means **the opposite of join?** (Signal.) *Disjoin.*
• What's word 3? (Signal.) *Appear.*
• What word means **the opposite of appear?** (Signal.) *Disappear.*
• What's word 4? (Signal.) *Charge.*
• What word means **the opposite of charge?** (Signal.) *Discharge.*

- Yes, if you **dis**charge a battery, you get rid of the charge it has. If you **re**charge a battery, you charge it up again.
f. Touch the line for word 1. ✔
- The word you'll write on that line means **the opposite of arrange.** Write the word that means **the opposite of arrange.** ✔
- Touch the line for word 2. ✔
- The word you'll write on that line means **to join again.** Write the word that means **to join again.** ✔
- Touch the line for word 3. ✔
- The word you'll write on that line means **to appear again.** Write the word that means **to appear again.** ✔
- Touch the line for word 4. ✔
- The word you'll write on that line means **the opposite of charge.** Write the word that means **the opposite of charge.** ✔
g. Check your work. Word 1. Everybody, what word means **the opposite of arrange?** (Signal.) *Disarrange.*
- Word 2. What word means **to join again?** (Signal.) *Rejoin.*
- Word 3. What word means **to appear again?** (Signal.) *Reappear.*
- Word 4. What word means **the opposite of charge?** (Signal.) *Discharge.*

EXERCISE 2
TOPICS

a. Find part B on your worksheet. ✔
- (Write on the board:)

Someone I Really Admire

- Here's the title for the story you're going to write in part B.
- Earlier, you wrote about people who you admire. This time, you're going to do it

without any help about the kind of sentences to write. You can write about one of the same people you wrote about earlier. Try to make your paper well organized and give good reasons for admiring this person. Make your paper interesting to read.
- Write your account. Raise your hand when you're finished.
(Observe students and give feedback.)
- (Students may do their writing and rewriting on a computer, using word-processing software.)
b. I'm going to call on individual students to read their account. I want you to listen carefully and do the following. Write down one or two questions you would like to ask the reader. Maybe you want to know more about where the reader was when the experience took place. Maybe you want to know more about what happened afterwards. Remember, write down one or more good questions.
- Then I want you to be prepared to tell what you think about the account. Tell about a part of it that you thought was interesting. Or tell what you think the reader could do to make the account more interesting.
c. (Collect papers. Mark mistakes in spelling and usage.)

EXERCISE 3
REWRITING

- (After you return the corrected papers, students are to write a final draft and possibly make an illustration for their account.)

Lesson 85

Materials: Each student will need a copy of the worksheets for lesson 85 (blackline masters 34 and 35).

EXERCISE 1
POEMS

Lesson 85

A. Make a poem from this story.

STORY	POEM
There once was a <u>king</u>. Ring was his name.	• There once was a king
He always carried so much <u>gold</u> that he looked elderly.	• He always carried so much gold,
The gold was so heavy he couldn't stand up <u>tall</u>. Sometimes, he would have to crawl around.	• He couldn't stand up tall.
He was a terrible <u>sight</u>. He called in a doctor late one evening.	• He was a terrible sight.
The doctor said his problem was he was carrying too much gold with <u>him</u>. So he weighed a lot, even though he was a slim man.	• The doctor said the king had too much gold on him.
So the king left his gold at home after that <u>night</u>. And from then on, he could stand up the right way.	• The king left his gold at home after that night.
Now his face is full of <u>smiles</u>. He can walk a long, long way.	• Now his face is full of smiles.

Note: For this activity, assign four students to each team. After forming groups, each team will make up its poem and read it to the rest of the class.

a. Find part A on your worksheet. ✔

• I'm going to read you the story. You're going to make up a poem from the story I tell you. This is a hard assignment. You'll have to think and do a lot of rewriting before you get your poem the way you want it.

b. I'll read the story. The poem you'll write will be a funny poem about a king. Here's a story about the king. Follow along:

> There once was a <u>king</u>. Ring was his name.
>
> He always carried so much <u>gold</u> that he looked elderly.
>
> The gold was so heavy he couldn't walk or stand up <u>tall</u>. Sometimes, he would have to crawl around.
>
> He was a terrible <u>sight</u>. He called in a doctor late one evening.
>
> The doctor said his problem was he was carrying too much gold with <u>him</u>. So he weighed a lot, even though he was a slim man.
>
> So the king left his gold at home after that <u>night</u>. And from then on, he could stand up the right way.
>
> Now his face is full of <u>smiles</u>. He can walk a long, long way.

c. The story doesn't have parts that rhyme, but some of the words are underlined. That means, you could use them as the last word in a line of the poem. The first part of what I read tells about the king's name and about his problem. What's the king's name? (Signal.) *Ring.*

- What's his problem? (Call on several students. Ideas: *He carried so much gold, he looked old. He couldn't do things.*)
- What were some of the things he couldn't do? (Call on several students. Ideas: *He couldn't stand up tall. He couldn't walk.*)

d. Listen. Start with this line: **There once was a king** and make up a line that rhymes. (Call on a student. Idea: *There once was a king. His name was [King]* **Ring.**)

e. Listen. **He always carried so much gold, that he looked elderly.** Start with **he always carried so much gold,** and make up another ending that rhymes. (Call on a student. Idea: *He always carried so much gold,* **that he looked [like he was very] old.**)

f. Your group is to make up lines that rhyme for the whole story. Remember, after you write two lines that rhyme with each other, you write two more lines that rhyme with each other. The last two lines do not have to rhyme with the first two lines. When you get lines that you like, somebody in the group should write them down. Raise your hand when your group is finished writing the poem.

g. (Observe and give feedback to groups as they work. If groups get stuck on parts of the poem, prompt them about how to create a pair of lines that rhyme.)

Answer Key:
There once was a <u>king</u>.
His name was **Ring.**

He always carried so much <u>gold</u>,
That he looked [very] **old.**

He couldn't stand up tall.
Sometimes he would [fall and] **crawl.**

He was a terrible <u>sight</u>.
He called a doctor late one **night.**

The doctor said the king had too much gold on <u>him</u>.
He weighed a lot even though he was **slim.**
The king left his gold at home after that <u>night</u>.

From then on he could stand up **right.**

Now his face is full of <u>smiles.</u>
He can walk for **miles and miles.**

Note: Other rhymes are possible. Not all groups should make up the same poem.

- (Do not require the same measure for lines that rhyme.)

h. Check to make sure your poem tells the whole story. Each member of your group is to copy the group's poem. Raise your hand when you're finished. (Observe students and give feedback.)

i. (Have each group read its poem to the entire class.)

- (You may require each group to memorize the group's poem and recite it to the class.)

85

EXERCISE 2
AFFIXES

Lesson 85		
B. 1	2	3
1. approve	_____	_____
2. arrange	_____	_____
3. order	_____	_____
4. join	_____	_____
5. connect	_____	_____

a. Find part B on your worksheet. ✔
- You're going to write words with the prefixes **dis** and **re**.
b. Everybody, what does the prefix **re** mean? (Signal.) *Again.*
- What does the prefix **dis** mean? (Signal.) *The opposite of.*
- (Repeat until firm.)
c. Touch word 1. ✔
- What's word 1? (Signal.) *Approve.*
- In column 2, write the word that means **the opposite of approve.** In column 3, write the word that means **to approve again.** Raise your hand when you're done. ✔
d. Everybody, what's word 2? (Signal.) *Arrange.*
- In column 2, write the word that means **to arrange again.** In column 3, write the word that means **the opposite of arrange.** Raise your hand when you're done. ✔
e. Everybody, what's word 3? (Signal.) *Order.*
- In column 2, write the word that means **to order again.** In column 3, write the word that means **the opposite of order.** Raise your hand when you're done. ✔
f. Everybody, what's word 4? (Signal.) *Join.*
- In column 2, write the word that means **the opposite of join.** In column 3, write the word that means **to join again.** Raise your hand when you're done. ✔
g. Everybody, what's word 5? (Signal.) *Connect.*
- In column 2, write the word that means **the opposite of connect.** In column 3, write the word that means **to connect again.** Raise your hand when you're done. ✔
h. Check your work. Word 1, column 2. Everybody what word means **the opposite of approve?** (Signal.) *Disapprove.*
- Word 1, column 3. What word means **to approve again?** (Signal.) *Reapprove.*
- Word 2, column 2. What word means **to arrange again?** (Signal.) *Rearrange.*
- Word 2, column 3. What word means **the opposite of arrange?** (Signal.) *Disarrange.*
- Yes, if you had things arranged and then you totally messed up the arrangement, you would disarrange the things.
- Word 3, column 2. What word means **to order again?** (Signal.) *Reorder.*
- Word 3, column 3. What word means **the opposite of order?** (Signal.) *Disorder.*
- Word 4, column 2. What word means **the opposite of join?** (Signal.) *Disjoin.*
- Word 4, column 3. What word means **to join again?** (Signal.) *Rejoin.*
- Word 5, column 2. What word means **the opposite of connect?** (Signal.) *Disconnect.*
- Word 5, column 3. What word means **to connect again?** (Signal.) *Reconnect.*

Materials: Each student will need a copy of the worksheet for lesson 86 (blackline master 35), lined paper, and illustrating materials.

EXERCISE 1
AFFIXES

Lesson 86		
1	2	3
1. join	_____	_____
2. order	_____	_____
3. charge	_____	_____
4. connect	_____	_____
5. continue	_____	_____

a. Find lesson 86 on your worksheet. ✔

• You're going to write words with the prefixes **dis** and **re.**

b. Everybody, what does the prefix **dis** mean? (Signal.) *The opposite of.*

• What does the prefix **re** mean? (Signal.) *Again.*

• (Repeat until firm.)

c. Touch the line for word 1. ✔

• What's word 1? (Signal.) *Join.*

• In column 2, write the word that means **the opposite of join.** In column 3, write the word that means **to join again.** Raise your hand when you're done. ✔

d. Everybody, what's word 2? (Signal.) *Order.*

• In column 2, write the word that means **to order again.** In column 3, write the word that means **the opposite of order.** Raise your hand when you're done. ✔

e. Everybody, what's word 3? (Signal.) *Charge.*

• In column 2, write the word that means **the opposite of charge.** In column 3, write the word that means **to charge again.** Raise your hand when you're done. ✔

f. Everybody, what's word 4? (Signal.) *Connect.*

• In column 2, write the word that means **to connect again.** In column 3, write

the word that means **the opposite of connect.** Raise your hand when you're done. ✔

g. Everybody, what's word 5? (Signal.) *Continue.*

• In column 2, write the word that means **to continue again.** In column 3, write the word that means **the opposite of continue.** Raise your hand when you're done. ✔

h. Check your work. Word 1, column 2. Everybody, what word means **the opposite of join?** (Signal.) *Disjoin.*

• Word 1, column 3. What word means **to join again?** (Signal.) *Rejoin.*

• Word 2, column 2. What word means **to order again?** (Signal.) *Reorder.*

• Word 2, column 3. What word means **the opposite of order?** (Signal.) *Disorder.*

• Word 3, column 2. What word means **the opposite of charge?** (Signal.) *Discharge.*

• Word 3, column 3. What word means **to charge again?** (Signal.) *Recharge.*

• Word 4, column 2. Everybody what word means **to connect again?** (Signal.) *Reconnect.*

• Word 4, column 3. What word means **the opposite of connect?** (Signal.) *Disconnect.*

• Word 5, column 2. What word means **to continue again?** (Signal.) *Recontinue.*

• Word 5, column 3. What word means **the opposite of continue?** (Signal.) *Discontinue.*

EXERCISE 2

TOPICS

a. (Write on the board:)

> **A Time Somebody Helped Me Out**

- Here's the title for your story.
- You're going to write about a time you needed help and somebody helped you. Maybe you needed money. Maybe you needed help with something you were trying to do. Think about a time when somebody really helped you out of a bad spot.

b. Listen: First you'll tell when somebody helped you and where you were. Then tell why you needed help and who helped you. Tell what the person did and what happened. End your story by telling what happened later. Write your account. Raise your hand when you're finished.

   (Observe students and give feedback.)

- (Students may do their writing and rewriting on a computer, using word-processing software.)

c. I'm going to call on individual students to read their account. I want you to listen carefully and do the following. Write down one or two questions you would like to ask the reader. Maybe you want to know more about where the reader was when the experience took place. Maybe you want to know more about what happened afterwards. Remember, write down one or more good questions.

- Then I want you to be prepared to tell what you think about the account. Tell about a part of it that you thought was interesting. Or tell what you think the reader could do to make the account more interesting.

- (Call individual students to read their account and other students to comment.)

d. (Collect papers and give feedback for changes. Mark sentences that do not have ending marks. Mark parts that do not tell what they are supposed to tell.)

EXERCISE 3

REWRITING

- (After you return the corrected papers, students are later to revise their papers and incorporate the changes you indicated. After students revise their reports, direct students to illustrate their reports with a picture that shows what happened. They may write labels for the people or things in the picture.)

Lesson 87

EXERCISE 1
AFFIXES

Lesson 87

A. Write the word for each description.

1. What word means **to tell again?** _____
2. What word means **not able?** _____
3. What word means **not broken?** _____
4. What word means **to play again?** _____
5. What word means **the opposite of continue?** _____
6. What word means **not buttoned?** _____

B. Make a poem from this story.

STORY	POEM
Cal was a big green <u>duck</u>. But Cal was not very lucky.	• Cal was a big green duck.
Things always went bad for <u>Cal</u>. Nobody wanted to be his friend.	• Things always went bad for Cal.
When Cal was around, things were never <u>good</u>. They never went the way they should go.	• When Cal was around, things were never good.
One day, there wasn't a cloud in the <u>sky</u>. As soon as Cal started to fly, clouds appeared all over.	• One day, there wasn't a cloud in the sky.
One duck said, "I'll make a <u>bet</u>. Before Cal lands, we'll all be covered with water."	• One duck said, "I'll make a bet.
That duck was absolutely <u>right</u>. Everything was flooded before the night was over.	• That duck was absolutely right.

---

a. (Write on the board:)

un

- You're going to write words that have a new prefix, **un. Un** means **not.** If something is unseen, it is not seen. If it is unfair, it is not fair.
b. Everybody, what does the word **unbroken** mean? (Signal.) *Not broken.*
- What does the word **unbuckled** mean? (Signal.) *Not buckled.*
- What does the word **unbeaten** mean? (Signal.) *Not beaten.*
c. Find part A on your worksheet. ✔
- (Tell the students when they should complete the items.)
d. (After the students complete the items, do a workcheck. For each item: Read the item. Call on a student to answer it. If the answer is wrong, say the correct answer.)

Answer Key: 1. retell **2.** unable **3.** unbroken **4.** replay **5.** discontinue **6.** unbuttoned

EXERCISE 2
POEMS

Note: For this activity, assign four students to each team. After forming groups, each team will make up its poem and read it to the rest of the class.

a. Find part B on your worksheet. ✔
- I'm going to read you the story. I'll read the first part today. You're going to make up a poem from the story I tell you. This is a hard assignment. You'll have to think and do a lot of rewriting before you get your poem the way you want it.
- I'll read the story. Follow along. This is the first part of the story:

Cal was a big green <u>duck</u>. But Cal was not very lucky.

Things always went bad for <u>Cal</u>. Nobody wanted to be his friend.

When Cal was around, things were never <u>good</u>. They never went the way they should go.

One day, there wasn't a cloud in the <u>sky</u>. As soon as Cal started to fly, clouds appeared all over.

One duck said, "I'll make a <u>bet</u>. Before Cal lands, we'll all be covered with water."

That duck was absolutely <u>right</u>. Everything was flooded before the night was over.

---

b. The first part of what I read tells about the duck and his problem. What's the duck's name? (Signal.) *Cal.*

• What's his problem? (Call on several students. Ideas: *He was not lucky. Things didn't go well when he was around.*)

• What was a bad thing that happened? (Call on several students. Ideas: *Flooding; clouds would appear.*)

c. Listen. Start with this line: **Cal was a big green duck** and make up a line that rhymes. (Call on a student. Idea: *Cal was a big green duck.* ***But Cal didn't have much luck.****)*

d. Listen. Here's another line: **Things always went bad for Cal.** Start with that line and make up another line that rhymes. (Call on a student. Idea: *Things always went bad for Cal.* ***Nobody wanted to be his pal.****)*

e. Listen. Here's another line: **When Cal was around things were never good.** Start with that line and make up another line that rhymes. (Call on a student. Idea: *When Cal was around, things were never good.* ***They never went the way they should.****)*

f. Your group is to make up lines that rhyme for the whole story. Remember, after you write two lines that rhyme with each other, you write two more lines that rhyme with each other. The last two lines do not have to rhyme with the first two lines. When you get lines that you like, somebody in the group should write them down. Raise your hand when your group is finished writing the poem.

g. (Observe and give feedback to groups as they work. If groups get stuck on parts of the poem, prompt them about how to create a pair of lines that rhyme.)

Answer Key:
Cal was a big green <u>duck</u>.
But Cal didn't have much **luck.**

Things always went bad for <u>Cal</u>.
Nobody wanted to be his **pal.**

When Cal was around, things were never <u>good</u>.
They never went the way they **should.**

One day, there wasn't a cloud in the <u>sky</u>.
But clouds appeared when Cal started to **fly.**

One duck said, "I'll make a <u>bet</u>.
Before Cal lands, we'll all be **wet."**

That duck was absolutely <u>right</u>.
Everything was flooded by the end of **night.**

Note: Other rhymes are possible. Not all groups should make up the same poem.

• (Do not require the same measure for lines that rhyme.)

h. Check to make sure your poem tells the whole story. Each member of your group is to copy the group's poem. Raise your hand when you're finished.
(Observe students and give feedback.)

i. (Have each group read its poem to the entire class.)

• (You may require each group to memorize the group's poem and recite it to the class.)

Note: The other part of this poem is introduced in lesson 88.

Lesson 88

Materials: Each student will need a copy of the worksheets for lesson 88 (blackline masters 37 and 38)

EXERCISE 1
POEMS

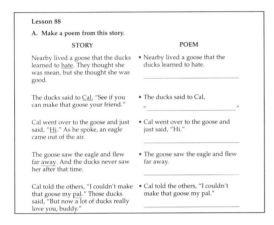

Note: For this activity, assign the same four-student teams.

a. Find part A on your worksheet. ✔
- You're going to write the second part of the poem about Cal. See what you remember about Cal. Was Cal lucky? (Signal.) *No.*
- If Cal wanted the weather to be sunny, what kind of weather would come in? (Call on a student. Idea: *Cloudy; rainy.*)

- If Cal tried to make friends with somebody, would he succeed? (Signal.) *No.*

b. I'll read the rest of the story. Follow along:

> Nearby lived a goose that the ducks learned to <u>hate</u>. They thought she was mean, but she thought she was good.
>
> The ducks said to <u>Cal</u>, "See if you can make that goose your friend."
>
> Cal went over to the goose and just said, "<u>Hi</u>." As he spoke, an eagle came out of the air.
>
> The goose saw the eagle and flew far <u>away</u>. And the ducks never saw her after that time.
>
> Cal told the others, "I couldn't make that goose my <u>pal</u>." Those ducks said, "But now a lot of ducks really love you, buddy."

c. Listen to the first line: **Nearby lived a goose that the ducks learned to hate.** Start with that line and make up another line that rhymes. (Call on a student. Idea: *Nearby lived a goose that the ducks learned to hate. **They thought she was mean, but she thought she was great.***)

d. Your group is to make up lines that rhyme for the whole story. Remember, after you write two lines that rhyme with each other, you write two more lines that rhyme with each other. The last two lines do not have to rhyme with the first two lines. When you get lines that you like, somebody in the group should write them down. Raise your hand when your group is finished writing the poem.

e. (Observe and give feedback to groups as they work. If groups get stuck on parts of the poem, prompt them about how to create a pair of lines that rhyme.)

Answer Key:

Nearby lived a goose that the ducks learned to hate.
They thought she was mean, but she thought she was **great.**

The ducks said to Cal,
"See if you can make that goose your **pal.**"

Cal went over to the goose and just said, "Hi."
As he spoke, an eagle came out of the **sky.**

The goose saw the eagle and flew far away.
And the ducks never saw her after that **day.**

Cal told the others, "I couldn't make that goose my pal."
Those ducks said, "But now a lot of ducks really love you, **Cal.**"

Note: Other rhymes as possible.

• (Do not require the same measure for each pair of lines that rhyme. As long as the measure is the same for both lines within a pair, the poem is acceptable.)

f. Check to make sure your poem tells the whole story. Each member of your group is to copy the group's poem. Raise your hand when you're finished.
(Observe students and give feedback.)

g. (Have each group read its poem [part 2 or both parts] to the entire class.)

• (You may require each group to memorize the group's poem and recite it to the class.)

EXERCISE 2
AFFIXES

B. Write the word for each description.
1. What word means **the opposite of appear?** _____
2. What word means **to approve again?** _____
3. What word means **not clean?** _____
4. What word means **not fair?** _____
5. What word means **the opposite of connect?** _____
6. What word means **not aware?** _____

a. Find part B on your worksheet. ✔
b. Everybody, what prefix means **again?** (Signal.) *Re.*
• What prefix means **the opposite of?** (Signal.) *Dis.*
• What prefix means **not?** (Signal.) *Un.*
• (Repeat step b until firm.)
c. What word means **not buckled?** (Signal.) *Unbuckled.*
d. *What word means* **not certain?** (Signal.) *Uncertain.*
e. (Tell the students when they should complete the items.)
f. (After the students complete the items, do a workcheck. For each item: Read the item. Call on a student to answer it. If the answer is wrong, say the correct answer.)

Answer Key: 1. disappear **2.** reapprove
3. unclean **4.** unfair **5.** disconnect
6. unaware

Materials: Each student will need a copy of the worksheet for lesson 89 (blackline master 38).

AFFIXES

> **Lesson 89**
>
> Write the word for each description.
>
> 1. What word means **without effort?** _____
> 2. What word means **without a home?** _____
> 3. What word means **the opposite of order?** _____
> 4. What word means **to order again?** _____
> 5. What word means **not zipped?** _____
> 6. What word means **without a hat?** _____

a. Find lesson 89 on your worksheet. ✔

• Some word parts appear at the beginning of a word. Everybody, what are those parts called? (Signal.) *Prefixes.*

• There are also parts that appear at the end of words. Those parts are called **suffixes.**

• What are parts at the end of words called? (Signal.) *Suffixes.*

• What are parts at the beginning of words called? (Signal.) *Prefixes.*

• (Repeat until firm.)

b. (Write on the board:)

> **less**

• The suffix spelled L-E-S-S means **without.** What does the suffix **less** mean? (Signal.) *Without.*

c. What word means **without hope?** (Signal.) *Hopeless.*

• What word means **without shoes?** (Signal.) *Shoeless.*

• What word means **without thought?** (Signal.) *Thoughtless.*

• (Repeat step c until firm.)

d. (Tell the students when they should complete the items.)

e. (After the students complete the items, do a workcheck. For each item: Read the item. Call on a student to answer it. If the answer is wrong, say the correct answer.)

Answer Key: 1. effortless **2.** homeless **3.** disorder **4.** reorder **5.** unzipped **6.** hatless

Lesson 90

Materials: Each student will need a copy of the worksheet for lesson 90 (blackline master 39).

AFFIXES

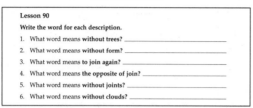

a. You've learned some prefixes and one suffix.

b. Everybody, which part goes at the beginning of a word? (Signal.) *Prefix.*
- Which part goes at the end of a word? (Signal.) *Suffix.*
- (Repeat step b until firm.)

c. What prefix means **again?** (Signal.) *Re.*
- What prefix means **not?** (Signal.) *Un.*

- What prefix means **the opposite of?** (Signal.) *Dis.*
- What suffix means **without?** (Signal.) *Less.*

d. (Tell the students when they should complete the items.)

e. (After the students complete the items, do a workcheck. For each item: Read the item. Call on a student to answer it. If the answer is wrong, say the correct answer.)

Answer Key: 1. treeless **2.** formless **3.** rejoin **4.** disjoin **5.** jointless **6.** cloudless

Materials: Each student will need a copy of the worksheet for lesson 91 (blackline master 39).

AFFIXES

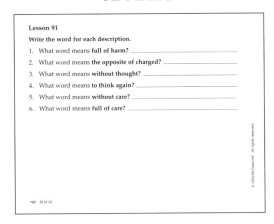

a. Find lesson 91 on your worksheet. ✔
• Some word parts appear at the beginning of words, and some word parts appear at the end of words.
b. What are parts at the beginning of words called? (Signal.) *Prefixes.*
• What are parts at the end of words called? (Signal.) *Suffixes.*
• (Repeat step b until firm.)
c. (Write on the board:)

ful

• The suffix spelled F-U-L means **full of.** What does the suffix **ful** mean? (Signal.) *Full of.*
d. Everybody, what word means **full of care?** (Signal.) *Careful.*
• What word means **full of hope?** (Signal.) *Hopeful.*
• (Repeat step d until firm.)
e. (Tell the students when they should complete the items.)
f. (After the students complete the items, do a workcheck. For each item: Read the item. Call on a student to answer it. If the answer is wrong, say the correct answer.)

Answer Key: 1. harmful **2.** discharged
3. thoughtless **4.** rethink **5.** careless
6. careful

Lesson 92

Materials: Each student will need a copy of the worksheet for lesson 92 (blackline master 40).

AFFIXES

Name _____

Lesson 92

Write the word for each description.

1. What word means **being hard?** _____
2. What word means **being tender?** _____
3. What word means **the opposite of belief?** _____
4. What word means **full of joy?** _____
5. What word means **without joy?** _____
6. What word means **being bright?** _____
7. What word means **not happy?** _____
8. What word means **without a shirt?** _____

a. Find lesson 92 on your worksheet. ✔
• Some word parts appear at the beginning of words, and some word parts appear at the end of words.
b. **What are parts at the end of words called?** (Signal.) *Suffixes.*
• What are parts at the beginning of words called? (Signal.) *Prefixes.*
• Is **less** a prefix or a suffix? (Signal.) *A suffix.*
• Is **dis** a prefix or a suffix? (Signal.) *A prefix.*
• (Repeat step b until firm.)
c. (Write on the board:)

ness

• The suffix spelled N-E-S-S means **being.** What does the suffix **ness** mean? (Signal.) *Being.*
• The word that means **being happy** is **happiness.**
d. What word means **being sad?** (Signal.) *Sadness.*
• What word means **being soft?** (Signal.) *Softness.*
• (Repeat step d until firm.)
e. (Tell the students when they should complete the items.)
f. (After the students complete the items, do a workcheck. For each item: Read the item. Call on a student to answer it. If the answer is wrong, say the correct answer.)

Answer Key: 1. hardness **2.** tenderness **3.** disbelief **4.** joyful **5.** joyless **6.** brightness **7.** unhappy **8.** shirtless

Lesson 93

Materials: Each student will need a copy of the worksheet for lesson 93 (blackline master 40).

AFFIXES

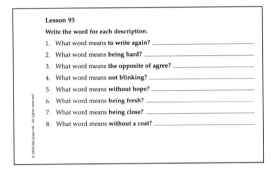

a. Find lesson 93 on your worksheet. ✔
b. Everybody, what are parts at the end of words called? **(Signal.)** *Suffixes.*
- What are parts at the beginning of words called? **(Signal.)** *Prefixes.*
- Is **un** a prefix or a suffix? **(Signal.)** *A prefix.*
- Is **ness** a prefix or a suffix? **(Signal.)** *A suffix.*
- (Repeat step b until firm.)

c. What suffix means **without? (Signal.)** *Less.*
- What suffix means **full of? (Signal.)** *Ful.*
- What suffix means **being? (Signal.)** *Ness.*
- (Repeat step c until firm.)

d. What word means **being empty?** **(Signal.)** *Emptiness.*
- What word means **being tasty?** (Signal.) *Tastiness.*
- (Repeat step d until firm.)
e. (Tell the students when they should complete the items.)
f. (After the students complete the items, do a workcheck. For each item: Read the item. Call on a student to answer it. If the answer is wrong, say the correct answer.)

Answer Key: 1. rewrite **2.** hardness **3.** disagree **4.** unblinking **5.** hopeless **6.** freshness **7.** closeness **8.** coatless

Lesson 94

Materials: Each student will need a copy of the worksheet for lesson 94 (blackline master 41).

AFFIXES

```
                    Name _____
Lesson 94
Write the word for each description.
  1. What word means one who rides? _____
  2. What word means being sad? _____
  3. What word means full of thought? _____
  4. What word means the opposite of approve? _____
  5. What word means one who runs? _____
  6. What word means without joy? _____
  7. What word means being dull? _____
  8. What word means not done? _____
  9. What word means without sleeves? _____
 10. What word means to read again? _____
```

a. Find lesson 94 on your worksheet. ✔
- Some word parts appear at the beginning of words, and some word parts appear at the end of words.

b. What are parts at the beginning of words called? (Signal.) *Prefixes.*
- What are parts at the end of words called? (Signal.) *Suffixes.*
- Is **ness** a prefix or a suffix? (Signal.) *A suffix.*
- Is **un** a prefix or a suffix? (Signal.) *A prefix.*
- Which suffix means **being**? (Signal.) *Ness.*
- Which suffix means **full of**? (Signal.) *Ful.*
- Which suffix means **without**? (Signal.) *Less.*
- (Repeat step b until firm.)

c. (Write on the board:)

er

- The suffix spelled E-R means **one that.** Everybody, what does the suffix **er** mean? (Signal.) *One that.*
- The word that means **one who thinks** is **thinker.**

d. What word means **one who eats?** (Signal.) *Eater.*
- What word means **one who bats?** (Signal.) *Batter.*

e. (Tell the students when they should complete the items.)

f. (After the students complete the items, do a workcheck. For each item: Read the item. Call on a student to answer it. If the answer is wrong, say the correct answer.)

Answer Key: 1. rider **2.** sadness **3.** thoughtful **4.** disapprove **5.** runner **6.** joyless **7.** dullness **8.** undone **9.** sleeveless **10.** reread

Materials: Each student will need a copy of the worksheet for lesson 95 (blackline master 42).

AFFIXES

Name _____

Lesson 95

Write the word for each description.

1. What word means **to type again?** _____
2. What word means **being cold?** _____
3. What word means **to wash again?** _____
4. What word means **one that washes?** _____
5. What word means **one that bakes?** _____
6. What word means **without taste?** _____
7. What word means **full of skill?** _____
8. What word means **being round?** _____
9. What word means **without care?** _____
10. What word means **one that tastes?** _____

BLM 42   163

a. Find lesson 95 on your worksheet. ✔
b. What suffix means **one that?** (Signal.) *Er.*
• What suffix means **without?** (Signal.) *Less.*
• What suffix means **full of?** (Signal.) *Ful.*
• What suffix means **being?** (Signal.) *Ness.*
• (Repeat step b until firm.)
c. (Tell the students when they should complete the items.)
d. (After the students complete the items, do a workcheck. For each item: Read the item. Call on a student to answer it. If the answer is wrong, say the correct answer.)

Answer Key: 1. retype **2.** coldness **3.** rewash **4.** washer **5.** baker **6.** tasteless **7.** skillful **8.** roundness **9.** careless **10.** taster

Lesson 96

Materials: Each student will need a copy of the worksheet for lesson 96 (blackline master 43).

AFFIXES

a. Find lesson 96 on your worksheet. ✔
b. Everybody, what are parts at the end of words called? (Signal.) *Suffixes.*
  • What are parts at the beginning of words called? (Signal.) *Prefixes.*
  • (Repeat step b until firm.)

c. (Write on the board:)

super

• The prefix spelled S-U-P-E-R means **very.** What does the prefix **super** mean? (Signal.) *Very.*
• The word that means **very clean** is **superclean.**
d. Everybody, what word means **very fine?** (Signal.) *Superfine.*
• What word means **very soft?** (Signal.) *Supersoft.*
• (Repeat step d until firm.)
e. (Tell the students when they should complete the items.)
f. (After the students complete the items, do a workcheck. For each item: Read the item. Call on a student to answer it. If the answer is wrong, say the correct answer.)

Answer Key: 1. hardness **2.** superhard **3.** coldness **4.** supercold **5.** discolored **6.** recolor **7.** tearful **8.** tearless **9.** brightness **10.** superbright **11.** unhealthy

Materials: Each student will need a copy of the worksheet for lesson 97 (blackline master 44).

AFFIXES

Name _____

Lesson 97

Write the word for each description.

1. What word means **one that sits?** _____
2. What word means **being narrow?** _____
3. What word means **without pain?** _____
4. What word means **being firm?** _____
5. What word means **very firm?** _____
6. What word means **not firm?** _____
7. What word means **one that gives?** _____
8. What word means **to give again?** _____
9. What word means **without water?** _____
10. What word means **very fast?** _____
11. What word means **one that speaks?** _____

BLM 44 166

a. Find lesson 97 on your worksheet. ✔

b. Everybody, what are parts at the end of words called? (Signal.) *Suffixes.*
- What are parts at the beginning of words called? (Signal.) *Prefixes.*
- Is **super** a prefix or a suffix? (Signal.) *A prefix.*
- Is **er** a prefix or a suffix? (Signal.) *A suffix.*
- Which prefix means **very?** (Signal.) *Super.*
- Which suffix means **the one that?** (Signal.) *Er.*
- Which suffix means **being?** (Signal.) *Ness.*
- Which suffix means **without?** (Signal.) *Less.*
- (Repeat step b until firm.)

c. (Tell the students when they should complete the items.)

d. (After the students complete the items, do a workcheck. For each item: Read the item. Call on a student to answer it. If the answer is wrong, say the correct answer.)

Answer Key: 1. sitter **2.** narrowness **3.** painless **4.** firmness **5.** superfirm **6.** unfirm **7.** giver **8.** regive **9.** waterless **10.** superfast **11.** speaker

Lesson 98

Materials: Each student will need a copy of the worksheet for lesson 98 (blackline master 45).

ALPHABETICAL ORDER

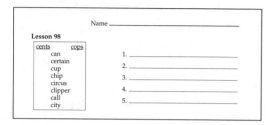

a. Find lesson 98 on your worksheet. ✔
- (Teacher reference:)

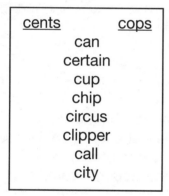

- The underlined words at the top of the box are **cents** and **cops**. Cents comes first in the alphabet. **Cops** comes later in the alphabet.
- Five of the words below come between **cents** and **cops** in the alphabet. Those words come after **cents** but before **cops**.

b. Write the five words that are between **cents** and **cops**. Write them in alphabetical order. For some of the words, the first two letters are the same, so you'll have to look at the third letter to see which is earlier in the alphabet. Raise your hand when you're finished. **(Observe students and give feedback.)**

c. (Write on the board:)

> 1. certain
> 2. chip
> 3. circus
> 4. city
> 5. clipper

- Check your work. Here's what you should have. Fix up any mistakes.

Lesson 99

ALPHABETICAL ORDER

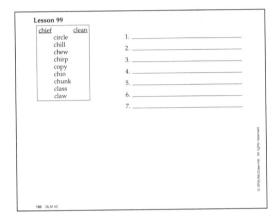

a. Find lesson 99 on your worksheet. ✔
• The underlined words at the top are **chief** and **clean.** Everybody, which word comes earlier in the alphabet? (Signal.) *Chief.*

b. Seven of the words below **chief** and **clean** come between them in the alphabet. Write the seven words in alphabetical order. Raise your hand when you're finished.
(Observe students and give feedback.)

c. (Write on the board:)

1. chill
2. chin
3. chirp
4. chunk
5. circle
6. class
7. claw

• Check your work. Here's what you should have. Fix up any mistakes.

Lesson 100

GLOSSARY AND GUIDE WORDS

Name _____

Lesson 100

Use the glossary in your book to answer the questions.

1. What are the guide words for the word **slight?** _____

2. What are the guide words for the word **crouch?** _____

---

a. Find page 343 in your textbook. ✔

- This part of the book is a glossary. A glossary gives meanings of words that are used in this book. The words are in alphabetical order. The two blue words at the top of each page are called guide words.

b. The first guide word on page 343 is **adults.** Everybody, touch that guide word. ✔

- That tells that the first word on page 343 is **adults.**

- Touch the other blue guide word for page 343. ✔

- Everybody, what's that guide word? (Signal.) *Arrange.*

- That tells that the last word on page 343 is **arrange.**

c. Turn to page 352. ✔

- Page 352 has two guide words. Everybody, touch the first guide word on that page. ✔

- What's the first guide word? (Signal.) *Koala.*

- So what's the first word on page 352? (Signal.) *Koala.*

- What's the second guide word on page 352? (Signal.) *Measure.*

- So what's the last word on that page? (Signal.) *Measure.*

d. (Write on the board:)

slight

- The word **slight** is on page 356 or page 357. If **slight** is on page 356, **slight** comes between **rich** and **soldiers** in the alphabet. If **slight** is on page 357, **slight** comes between **soundly** and **swoop** in the alphabet.

- Everybody, write the guide words for the page where you would find **slight.** (Observe students and give feedback.)

- Everybody, what are the guide words for **slight?** (Signal.) *Rich and soldiers.*

e. (Write on the board:)

crouch

- You'll write the guide words for the page **crouch** is on. If **crouch** is on page 345, **crouch** comes between **broiled** and **coconuts** in the alphabet. If **crouch** is on page 346, **crouch** comes between **Columbus** and **damage** in the alphabet.

- Everybody, write the guide words for the page where you would find **crouch.** (Observe students and give feedback.)

- Everybody, what are the guide words for **crouch?** (Signal.) *Columbus and damage.*

Lesson 101

Materials: Each student will need a copy of the worksheet for lesson 101 (blackline master 46).

GUIDE WORDS

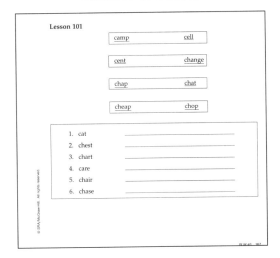

a. Find lesson 101 on your worksheet. ✔
- (Teacher reference:)

- Each row shows two guide words for pages in a glossary. The first guide words are **camp** and **cell.** The next guide words are **cent** and **change.** The next guide words are **chap** and **chat.** The last guide words are **cheap** and **chop.**
b. In the box below the guide words is a list of six words. Each of those words would go on a page that has one pair of the guide words.
- After each word in the box, you'll write the guide words for the page where you would find that word in the glossary.
- Word 1 is **cat. Cat** is between one pair of guide words. Find that pair and write them after the word **cat.** Raise your hand when you've done that much. **(Observe students and give feedback.)**
- Check your work. Everybody, what are the guide words for the word **cat?** (Signal.) *Camp and cell.*
- Yes, **cat** is between **camp** and **cell** in the alphabet.
c. Word 2 is **chest.** Figure out the guide words for the page where you'd find **chest** and write them after the word **chest.** Then do the guide words for the rest of the items. Raise your hand when you're finished. **(Observe students and give feedback.)**
d. (Write on the board:)

1. cat	camp	cell
2. chest	cheap	chop
3. chart	chap	chat
4. care	camp	cell
5. chair	cent	change
6. chase	chap	chat

- Check your work. Here's what you should have. Fix up any mistakes.

Lesson 102

Materials: Each student will need a copy of the worksheet for lesson 102 (blackline master 47).

GUIDE WORDS

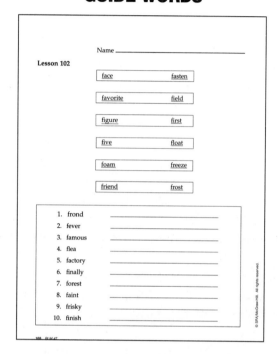

a. Find lesson 102 on your worksheet. ✔

• Each row shows guide words for six pages of a glossary. In the box are ten words that go on these pages.

b. After each word in the box, write the guide words for the page where you would find the word in a glossary. Raise your hand when you're finished. (Observe students and give feedback.)

c. (After the students complete the items, do a workcheck. For each item, call on a student to read the item and its guide words. If the answer is wrong, say the correct answer.)

Answer Key: 1. friend/frost **2.** favorite/field **3.** face/fasten **4.** five/float **5.** face/fasten **6.** figure/first **7.** foam/freeze **8.** face/fasten **9.** friend/frost **10.** figure/first

Lesson **103**

Materials: Each student will need a copy of the worksheet for lesson 103 (blackline master 48).

GUIDE WORDS

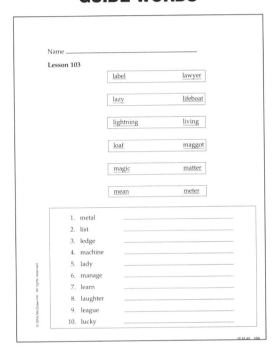

a. Find lesson 103 on your worksheet. ✔
• Each row shows guide words for six pages of a glossary. In the box are ten words that go on these pages.
b. After each word in the box, write the guide words for the page where you would find the word in a glossary. Raise your hand when you're finished. (Observe students and give feedback.)
c. (After the students complete the items, do a workcheck. For each item, call on a student to read the item and its guide words. If the answer is wrong, say the correct answer.)

Answer Key: 1. mean/meter
2. lightning/living **3.** lazy/lifeboat
4. loaf/maggot **5.** label/lawyer
6. magic/matter **7.** lazy/lifeboat
8. label/lawyer **9.** lazy/lifeboat
10. loaf/maggot

Lesson 104

Materials: Each student will need a copy of the worksheet for lesson 104 (blackline master 49).

ROOT WORDS

```
                    Name _____
Lesson 104

A. For each word, underline the prefix. Circle the root. Make a line over
   the suffix.
     1. return            4. brightness

     2. baker             5. disappear

     3. superclean        6. recliner

B. For each item, write the guide words that are on the correct page of
   the glossary in your textbook.
         Word                    Guide Words
     1. engine            _____
     2. adventure         _____
     3. gust              _____
```

a. (Write on the board:)

1. **return**	4. **brightness**
2. **disappear**	5. **baker**
3. **superclean**	6. **recliner**

- These are words you're going to work with.
- b. You add prefixes or suffixes to a part that's called a **root.** Everybody, what do you add prefixes or suffixes to? (Signal.) *A root.*
- Sometimes the root is a word. Sometimes it isn't.
- c. Word 1 is **return.** Everybody, what word? (Signal.) *Return.*
- Does it have a prefix? (Signal.) *Yes.*
- What's the prefix? (Signal.) *Re.*
- What's the root? (Signal.) *Turn.*

d. Word 2 is **disappear.** What word? (Signal.) *Disappear.*
- Does it have a prefix? (Signal.) *Yes.*
- What's the prefix? (Signal.) *Dis.*
- What's the root? (Signal.) *Appear.*
e. Word 3 is **superclean.** What word? (Signal.) *Superclean.*
- Does it have a prefix? (Signal.) *Yes.*
- What's the prefix? (Signal.) *Super.*
- What's the root? (Signal.) *Clean.*
f. Word 4 is **brightness.** What word? (Signal.) *Brightness.*
- Does it have a prefix? (Signal.) *No.*
- Does it have a suffix? (Signal.) *Yes.*
- What's the suffix? (Signal.) *Ness.*
- What's the root? (Signal.) *Bright.*
g. Word 5 is **baker.** What word? (Signal.) *Baker.*
- Does it have a prefix? (Signal.) *No.*
- Does it have a suffix? (Signal.) *Yes.*
- What's the suffix? (Signal.) *Er.*
- What's the root? (Signal.) *Bake.*
h. Word 6 is **recliner.** What word? (Signal.) *Recliner.*
- Does it have a prefix? (Signal.) *Yes.*
- What's the prefix? (Signal.) *Re.*
- Does it have a suffix? (Signal.) *Yes.*
- What's the suffix? (Signal.) *Er.*
- What's the root? (Signal.) *Cline.*
- That root is not a word.
i. Find part A on your worksheet. ✔
- These are the words we just did. The directions tell you to underline the prefix. Circle the root. Make a line over the suffix. Remember, each word has a root. So you'll circle something in each word.
j. (Tell the students when they should complete the items for parts A and B.)

k. (After the students complete the items, do a workcheck. For part A, call on a student for each item and ask: What root did you circle? What prefix did you underline? What suffix did you make a line over?)

• (For each item in part B, call on a student to read the item and its guide words. If the answer is wrong, say the correct answer.)

Answer Key: Part A: 1. re (turn) **2.** (bake)r̄ or (bak)ēr **3.** super (clean) **4.** (bright)n̄ess **5.** dis (appear) **6.** re (cline)r̄ or re (clin)ēr

Part B: 1. engine: earth, explain
2. adventure: adults, arrange **3.** gust: globe, honest

Lesson 105

ROOT WORDS

Name _____

Lesson 105

A. For each word, underline the prefix. Circle the root. Make a line over the suffix.

1. helpful
2. result
3. retain
4. contain
5. disable
6. unhappiness
7. sustainable

B. For each item, write the guide words that are on the correct page of the glossary in your textbook.

Word	Guide Words
1. constantly	
2. imitate	
3. mention	

BLM 50   171

a. (Write on the board:)

1. **result**	5. **retain**
2. **disable**	6. **contain**
3. **helpful**	7. **sustainable**
4. **unhappiness**	

- These are words you're going to work with.
b. You add prefixes or suffixes to a part of a word. Everybody, what do we call the part of a word you add prefixes or suffixes to? (Signal.) *Root.*
- Sometimes the root is a word. Sometimes it isn't.
c. Word 1 is **result.** Everybody, what word? (Signal.) *Result.*
- Does it have a prefix? (Signal.) *Yes.*
- What's the prefix? (Signal.) *Re.*

- What's the root? (Signal.) *Sult.*
- Is **sult** a word? (Signal.) *No.*
d. Word 2 is **disable.** What word? (Signal.) *Disable.*
- Does it have a prefix? (Signal.) *Yes.*
- What's the prefix? (Signal.) *Dis.*
- What's the root? (Signal.) *Able.*
e. Word 3 is **helpful.** What word? (Signal.) *Helpful.*
- Does it have a prefix? (Signal.) *No.*
- Does it have a suffix? (Signal.) *Yes.*
- What's the suffix? (Signal.) *Ful.*
- What's the root? (Signal.) *Help.*
f. Word 4 is **unhappiness.** What word? (Signal.) *Unhappiness.*
- Does it have a prefix? (Signal.) *Yes.*
- What's the prefix? (Signal.) *Un.*
- Does it have a suffix? (Signal.) *Yes.*
- What's the suffix? (Signal.) *Ness.*
- What's the root? (Signal.) *Happy.*
g. If you know the root, you can figure out what the prefixes and suffixes are. Word 5 is **retain.** What word? (Signal.) *Retain.*
- Does it have a prefix? (Signal.) *Yes.*
- What's the prefix? (Signal.) *Re.*
- Does it have a suffix? (Signal.) *No.*
- What's the root? (Signal.) *Tain.*
h. Word 6 has the same root: **contain.** What word? (Signal.) *Contain.*
- What's the root in that word? (Signal.) *Tain.*
- Is the rest of the word a **prefix** or a **suffix?** (Signal.) *Prefix.*
- What's the prefix? (Signal.) *Con.*
i. Word 7 has the same root. It has a prefix **and** a suffix. The word is **sustainable.** What word? (Signal.) *Sustainable.*
- What's the root? (Signal.) *Tain.*
- What's the prefix? (Signal.) *Sus.*

- What's the suffix? (Signal.) *Able.*
j. Find part A on your worksheet. ✔
- These are the words we just did. The directions tell you to underline the prefix. Circle the root. Make a line over the suffix. Remember, each word has a root. So you'll circle something in each word.
k. (Tell the students when they should complete the items for parts A and B.)
l. (After the students complete the items, do a workcheck. For part A, call on a student for each item and ask: What root did you circle? What prefix did you underline? What suffix did you make a line over?)

- (For each item in part B, call on a student to read the item and its guide words. If the answer is wrong, say the correct answer.)

Answer Key: Part A: 1. (help) f̅u̅l̅
2. re (sult) **3.** re (tain) **4.** con (tain) **5.** dis (able)
6. un (happi) n̅e̅s̅s̅ **7.** sus (tain) able

Part B: 1. constantly: Columbus, damage
2. imitate: hooves, Kennedy Airport
3. mention: mention, outcome

Lesson 106

Materials: Each student will need a copy of the worksheet for lesson 106 (blackline master 51).

ROOT WORDS

Name _____

Lesson 106

A. For each word, underline the prefix. Circle the root. Make a line over the suffix.

1. subjective
2. injection
3. detainment
4. reject
5. projection
6. revert
7. inverted

B. For each item, write the guide words that are on the correct page of the glossary in your textbook.

Word	Guide Words
1. drifts	_____
2. occasional	_____
3. cargo	_____

172 *BLM 51*

a. (Write on the board:)

1. detainment	**5. subjective**
2. reject	**6. revert**
3. injection	**7. inverted**
4. projection	

- These are words you're going to work with.
b. Everybody, what do we call the part of a word you add prefixes or suffixes to? (Signal.) *Root.*
c. If you know a root, you can figure out prefixes and suffixes of new words. Last time, you learned the root in the word **contain.** Everybody what's that root? (Signal.) *Tain.*

d. Word 1 is a word that has the same root: **detainment.** What word? (Signal.) *Detainment.*
- It has a prefix and a suffix. What's the prefix? (Signal.) *De.*
- What's the suffix? (Signal.) *Ment.*
- What's the root? (Signal.) *Tain.*
e. Word 2 is **reject.** What word? (Signal.) *Reject.*
- It has a root and a prefix. What's the root? (Signal.) *Ject.*
- What's the prefix? (Signal.) *Re.*
f. Word 3 has the same root: **injection.** What word? (Signal.) *Injection.*
- What's the prefix? (Signal.) *In.*
- What's the suffix? (Signal.) *Tion.*
- What's the root? (Signal.) *Ject.*
g. Word 4 has the same root: **projection.** What word? (Signal.) *Projection.*
- What's the prefix? (Signal.) *Pro.*
- What's the suffix? (Signal.) *Tion.*
- What's the root? (Signal.) *Ject.*
h. Word 5 has the same root: **subjective.** What word? (Signal.) *Subjective.*
- What's the prefix? (Signal.) *Sub.*
- What's the suffix? (Signal.) *Ive.*
- What's the root? (Signal.) *Ject.*
i. Word 6 is **revert.** What word? (Signal.) *Revert.*
- The word has a prefix and a root. What's the prefix? (Signal.) *Re.*
- What's the root? (Signal.) *Vert.*
j. Word 7 has the same root: **Inverted.** What word? (Signal.) *Inverted.*
- What's the prefix? (Signal.) *In.*
- What's the suffix? (Signal.) *Ed.*
- What's the root? (Signal.) *Vert.*

k. Find part A on your worksheet. ✔
• These are the words we just did. The directions tell you to underline the prefix. Circle the root. Make a line over the suffix. Remember, each word has a root. So you'll circle something in each word.
l. (Tell the students when they should complete the items for parts A and B.)
m. (After the students complete the items, do a workcheck. For part A, call on a student for each item and ask: What root did you circle? What prefix did you underline? What suffix did you make a line over?)

• (For each item in part B, call on a student to read the item and its guide words. If the answer is wrong, say the correct answer.)

Answer Key: Part A: 1. sub(ject)ive
2. in(jec)tion or in(ject)ion **3.** de(tain)ment
4. re(ject) **5.** pro(jec)tion or pro(ject)ion
6. re(vert) **7.** in(vert)ed

Part B: 1. drifts: danger, earplugs
2. occasional: mention, outcome **3.** cargo: broiled, coconuts

Lesson 107

Materials: Each student will need a copy of the worksheet for lesson 107 (blackline master 52).

ROOT WORDS

Name _____

Lesson 107

A. For each word, underline the prefix. Circle the root. Make a line over the suffix.

1. produce
2. reply
3. implicate
4. compliance
5. diverting
6. supplier
7. reducing

B. For each item, write the guide words that are on the correct page of the glossary in your textbook.

Word	Guide Words
1. frequently	_____
2. approach	_____
3. magnet	_____

BLM 52   173

a. (Write on the board:)

1. **diverting**	5. **implicate**
2. **reply**	6. **produce**
3. **compliance**	7. **reducing**
4. **supplier**	

- These are words you're going to work with.

b. Everybody, what do we call the part of a word you add prefixes or suffixes to? (Signal.) *Root.*

c. If you know a root, you can figure out prefixes and suffixes of new words. Last time, you learned the root in the word **inverted.** What's that root? (Signal.) *Vert.*

d. Word 1 is a word that has the same root: **diverting.** What word? (Signal.) *Diverting.*

- It has a prefix and a suffix. What's the prefix? (Signal.) *Di.*
- What's the suffix? (Signal.) *Ing.*

e. Word 2 is **reply.** What word? (Signal.) *Reply.*

- It has a root and a prefix. What's the prefix? (Signal.) *Re.*
- What's the root? (Signal.) *Ply.*

f. Word 3 has the same root: **compliance.** What word? (Signal.) *Compliance.*

- What's the prefix? (Signal.) *Com.*
- What's the suffix? (Signal.) *Ance.*
- What's the root? (Signal.) *Ply.*

g. Word 4 has the same root: **supplier.** What word? (Signal.) *Supplier.*

- What's the prefix? (Signal.) *Sup.*
- What's the suffix? (Signal.) *Er.*
- What's the root? (Signal.) *Ply.*

h. Word 5 has the same root: **implicate.** What word? (Signal.) *Implicate.*

- What's the prefix? (Signal.) *Im.*
- What's the suffix? (Signal.) *Cate.*
- What's the root? (Signal.) *Ply.*

i. Word 6 is **produce.** What word? (Signal.) *Produce.*

- The word has a prefix and a root. What's the prefix? (Signal.) *Pro.*
- What's the root? (Signal.) *Duce.*

j. Word 7 has the same root: **reducing.** What word? (Signal.) *Reducing.*

- What's the prefix? (Signal.) *Re.*
- What's the suffix? (Signal.) *Ing.*
- What's the root? (Signal.) *Duce.*

k. Find part A on your worksheet. ✔
- These are the words we just did. The directions tell you to underline the prefix. Circle the root. Make a line over the suffix. Remember, each word has a root. So you'll circle something in each word.
l. (Tell the students when they should complete the items for parts A and B.)
m. (After the students complete the items, do a workcheck. For part A, call on a student for each item and ask: What root did you circle? What prefix did you underline? What suffix did you make a line over?)

- (For each item in part B, call on a student to read the item and its guide words. If the answer is wrong, say the correct answer.)

Answer Key: Part A: 1. pro(duce) **2.** re(ply) **3.** im(pli)cate **4.** com(pli)ance **5.** di(vert)ing **6.** sup(pli)er **7.** re(duc)ing

Part B: 1. frequently: expression, gift **2.** approach: adults, arrange **3.** magnet: koala, measure

Lesson 108

Materials: Each student will need a copy of the worksheet for lesson 108 (blackline master 53); the teacher and each student will need a copy of the same children's dictionary.

DICTIONARY SKILLS

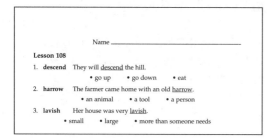

a. (Hold up a dictionary.) This is a dictionary. It tells what words mean.
- The words in a dictionary are in alphabetical order. The words on the first pages of the dictionary begin with **A.** The words at the end of the dictionary begin with **Z.**

b. Each page has guide words at the top. Open your dictionary to page 100. ✔
- Everybody, what are the guide words for page 100? (Signal.) (Accept appropriate response.)
- Open your dictionary to page 200. ✔
- What are the guide words for page 200? (Signal.) (Accept appropriate response.)
- What are the guide words for page 201? (Signal.) (Accept appropriate response.)

c. Find lesson 108 on your worksheet. ✔
- Word 1 is **descend.** Here's a sentence that uses the word **descend:** They will descend the hill. From that sentence, you don't know exactly what the word means. It could mean go up the hill or it could mean go down the hill, or it could mean they will eat the hill.
- Look up the word **descend** in the dictionary and read what it says after the word **descend.** Don't pay any attention to the letters and funny marks that come after the word **descend.** Just keep reading and you'll find out what **descend** means. You don't have to read the whole thing. Then circle what **descend** means.
(Observe students and give feedback.)
- What does **descend** mean? (Call on a student.) *Go down.*
- Everybody, touch the word **descend** in the dictionary. ✔
- I'll read the sentence that tells what **descend** means. (Read the first definition.)

d. Word 2 is **harrow.** Here's a sentence that uses the word **harrow:** The farmer came home with an old harrow. A harrow could be an animal, a tool, or a person. Look up **harrow** and circle whether it's an animal, a tool, or a person.
(Observe students and give feedback.)
- Everybody, is a harrow an animal, a tool, or a person? (Signal.) *A tool.*

e. Word 3 is **lavish.** Here's a sentence that uses the word **lavish:** Her house was very lavish. **Lavish** could mean **small,** or **large,** or it could be much more house than she needs. Look up the word **lavish** and circle what it means. **(Observe students and give feedback.)**

• Everybody, does lavish mean **small, large,** or **more than someone needs?** (Signal.) *More than someone needs.*

Lesson 109

Materials: Each student will need a copy of the worksheet for lesson 109 (blackline master 53); the teacher and each student will need a copy of the same children's dictionary.

DICTIONARY SKILLS

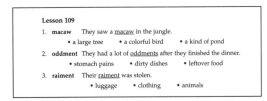

Lesson 109
1. **macaw**   They saw a <u>macaw</u> in the jungle.
   • a large tree   • a colorful bird   • a kind of pond
2. **oddment** They had a lot of <u>oddments</u> after they finished the dinner.
   • stomach pains   • dirty dishes   • leftover food
3. **raiment** Their <u>raiment</u> was stolen.
        • luggage   • clothing   • animals

a. (Hold up a dictionary.) Everybody, what kind of book is this? (Signal.) *Dictionary.*
• The dictionary gives meanings of words. Remember, the words in a dictionary are in alphabetical order. The words on the first pages of the dictionary begin with **A.** The words at the end of the dictionary begin with **Z.**
b. Find lesson 109 on your worksheet. ✔
• Word 1 is **macaw.** Here's a sentence that uses the word **macaw:** They saw a macaw in the jungle. From that sentence, you don't know exactly what the word means. A macaw could be a large tree, a colorful bird, or a kind of pond. Look up the word **macaw** in the dictionary and read what it says after the word **macaw.** Then circle what **macaw** means.
(Observe students and give feedback.)

c. Everybody, what is a macaw? (Signal.) *A colorful bird.*
• Touch the word **macaw** in the dictionary. ✔
• I'll read the sentence that tells what a macaw is. (Read the first definition.)
d. Word 2 is **oddment.** Here's a sentence that uses the word **oddment:** They had a lot of oddments after they finished the dinner. Oddments could be stomach pains, dirty dishes, or leftover food. Look up **oddment** and circle what it is. (Observe students and give feedback.)
• Everybody, are oddments stomach pains, dirty dishes, or leftover food? (Signal.) *Leftover food.*
e. Word 3 is **raiment.** Here's a sentence that uses the word **raiment:** Their raiment was stolen. Their raiment could be their luggage, or their clothing, or their animals. Look up the word **raiment** and circle what it means.
(Observe students and give feedback.)
• Everybody, is raiment their luggage, their clothing, or their animals? (Signal.) *Their clothing.*

Materials: Each student will need a copy of the worksheet for lesson 110 (blackline master 54); the teacher and each student will need a copy of the same children's dictionary.

DICTIONARY SKILLS

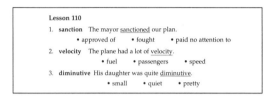

Lesson 110

1. **sanction**   The mayor <u>sanctioned</u> our plan.
   • approved of   • fought   • paid no attention to
2. **velocity**   The plane had a lot of <u>velocity</u>.
   • fuel   • passengers   • speed
3. **diminutive**   His daughter was quite <u>diminutive</u>.
   • small   • quiet   • pretty

a. (Hold up a dictionary.) Everybody, what kind of book is this? (Signal.) *Dictionary.*

• You're going to look up words and write what they mean.

b. Find lesson 110 on your worksheet. ✔

• Word 1 is **sanction.** Here's a sentence that uses the word **sanction:** The mayor sanctioned our plan. From that sentence, you don't know exactly what the word means. The mayor could approve of our plan, fight our plan, or pay no attention to our plan.

• Look up the word **sanction** in the dictionary and circle whether the mayor approved of our plan, fought the plan or paid no attention to the plan.
(Observe students and give feedback.)

c. Everybody, if the mayor sanctioned the plan, what did the mayor do? (Signal.) *Approved of the plan.*

• I'll read the sentence in the dictionary that tells what the mayor did. (Read the first definition for the **verb** sanction.)

d. Word 2 is **velocity.** What word? (Signal.) *Velocity.*

• Here's a sentence that uses the word **velocity:** The plane had a lot of velocity. From that sentence **velocity** could mean that the plane had a lot of fuel, a lot of passengers, or a lot of speed. Look up **velocity** and circle what it means.
(Observe students and give feedback.)

• Everybody, did the plane have a lot of fuel, a lot of passengers, or a lot of speed? (Signal.) *A lot of speed.*

e. Word 3 is **diminutive.** What word? (Signal.) *Diminutive.*

• Here's a sentence that uses the word **diminutive:** His daughter was quite diminutive. From that sentence, she could be quite small, quite quiet, or quite pretty. Look up **diminutive** and circle what it means.
(Observe students and give feedback.)

• Everybody, was his daughter quite small, quite quiet, or quite pretty? (Signal.) *Quite small.*

Lesson 111

DICTIONARY SKILLS

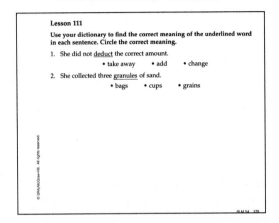

Lesson 111

Use your dictionary to find the correct meaning of the underlined word in each sentence. Circle the correct meaning.

1. She did not <u>deduct</u> the correct amount.
   • take away   • add   • change
2. She collected three <u>granules</u> of sand.
   • bags   • cups   • grains

a. Find lesson 111 on your worksheet. ✔

• For each item, you'll look up the underlined word in the dictionary. After you have found the word, read the choices that the item gives. Then read the definition that the dictionary gives and see which choice is correct.

b. Item 1: She did not deduct the correct amount. The choices are **take away, add,** or **change.** Look up the word **deduct** in your dictionary. Raise your hand when you've found it.
(Observe students and give feedback.)

• Read the choices for the item to yourself. Then read the definition to yourself and figure out which choice is correct. Circle that choice.
(Observe students and give feedback.)

• Everybody, when you deduct an amount, do you take away, add, or change the amount? **(Signal.)** *Take away.*

• You should have circled **take away.**

c. Read item 2 to yourself. Look up the word in the dictionary. Read the choices to yourself. Then read the definition the dictionary gives. Raise your hand when you've circled the correct choice.
(Observe students and give feedback.)

• Everybody, what are granules of sand— bags of sand, cups of sand, or grains of sand? **(Signal.)** *Grains of sand.*

• You should have circled **grains.**

Lesson 112

Materials: Each student will need a copy of the worksheet for lesson 112 (blackline master 55); the teacher and each student will need a copy of the same children's dictionary.

IDIOMATIC EXPRESSIONS

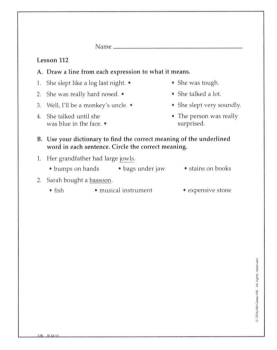

Name _____

Lesson 112

A. Draw a line from each expression to what it means.

1. She slept like a log last night. •   • She was tough.
2. She was really hard nosed. •   • She talked a lot.
3. Well, I'll be a monkey's uncle. •   • She slept very soundly.
4. She talked until she   • The person was really
   was blue in the face. •   surprised.

B. Use your dictionary to find the correct meaning of the underlined word in each sentence. Circle the correct meaning.

1. Her grandfather had large jowls.
   • bumps on hands   • bags under jaw   • stains on books
2. Sarah bought a bassoon.
   • fish   • musical instrument   • expensive stone

176   BLM 55

a. Some expressions don't mean what the words say. Here's an expression: He was really hard-nosed. Everybody, does that mean that his nose was hard, likc a board? (Signal.) *No.*
- What does it mean? (Call on a student. Ideas: *He was tough; he didn't give in easily.*)

b. Here's another expression that doesn't mean what the words say: She talked until she was blue in the face. Everybody, does that expression mean that she actually turned blue? (Signal.) *No.*

- What does it mean? (Call on a student. Ideas: *She talked a lot; she wouldn't stop talking.*)

c. Here's another expression that doesn't mean what the words say: Well, I'll be a monkey's uncle. Everybody, does that mean the speaker is related to a monkey? (Signal.) *No.*
- What does it mean? (Call on a student. Ideas: *The person is really surprised; the person has trouble believing something that he found out.*)

d. Here's another expression that doesn't mean what the words say: He slept like a log last night. Everybody, does that mean that he was like a log? (Signal.) *No.*
- What does it mean? (Call on a student. Idea: *He slept very soundly.*)

e. Find part A on your worksheet. ✔
- These are the expressions we just went over. You're going to draw a line from each expression to what it means.

f. (Tell the students when they should complete the items for parts A and B.)

g. (After the students complete the items, do a workcheck. For each item: Read the item. Call on a student to answer it. If the answer is wrong, say the correct answer.)

Answer Key: Part A: 1. She slept very soundly. **2.** She was tough. **3.** The person was really surprised. **4.** She talked a lot.

Part B: 1. jowls—bags under jaw
2. bassoon—musical instrument

Lesson 113

Materials: Each student will need a copy of the worksheet for lesson 113 (blackline master 56); the teacher and each student will need a copy of the same children's dictionary.

IDIOMATIC EXPRESSIONS

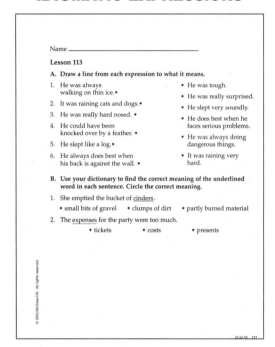

a. Some expressions don't mean what the words say. Here's an expression: He was always walking on thin ice. Everybody, does that mean that he was really on ice? (Signal.) *No.*
• What does it mean? (Call on a student. Idea: *He was always doing dangerous things.*)
b. Here's another expression that doesn't mean what the words say: He always does best when his back is against the wall. Everybody, does that expression mean that he is actually standing near a wall? (Signal.) *No.*
• What does it mean? (Call on a student. Ideas: *He does best when he faces very serious problems; the more difficult it is for him to succeed, the better he does.*)

c. Here's another expression that doesn't mean what the words say: He could have been knocked over by a feather. Everybody, does that mean he is that weak? (Signal.) *No.*
• What does it mean? (Call on a student. Idea: *He is really surprised.*)
d. Here's another expression that doesn't mean what the words say: It was raining cats and dogs. Everybody, does that mean that animals were coming out of the sky? (Signal.) *No.*
• What does it mean? (Call on a student. Idea: *It was raining very hard.*)
e. Find part A on your worksheet. ✔
• These are the expressions we just went over. You're going to draw a line from each expression to what it means.
f. (Tell the students when they should complete the items in parts A and B.)
g. (After the students complete the items, do a workcheck. For each item: Read the item. Call on a student to answer it. If the answer is wrong, say the correct answer.)

Answer Key: Part A: 1. He was always doing dangerous things. **2.** It was raining very hard. **3.** He was tough. **4.** He was really surprised. **5.** He slept very soundly. **6.** He does best when he faces serious problems.

Part B: 1. cinders—partly burned material **2.** expenses—costs

Lesson 114

SIMILES

Name _____

Lesson 114

A. Answer the questions about each simile.
- Her teeth were like pearls.
1. What two things are the same? _____
2. How were her teeth like pearls? _____
- Her eyes were as big as saucers.
3. What two things are the same? _____
4. What's the same about her eyes and saucers? _____
- Uncle Charlie moved like a bear.
5. What two things are the same? _____
6. What's the same about the way Uncle Charlie and a bear moved? _____
- The palm of his hand was like sandpaper.
7. What two things are the same? _____
8. What's the same about his hands and sandpaper? _____

B. Use your dictionary to find the correct meaning of the underlined word in each sentence. Circle the correct meaning.
1. The snow was <u>glistening</u> in the sunlight.
   - shining   - melting   - falling
2. Three <u>husky</u> men took a nap.
   - tired   - tall and thin   - big and strong

a. Some expressions are called similes. A simile names two things that are the same. A simile uses the word **like** or the word **as.** Everybody, what words do similes use? (Signal.) *Like or as.*

b. Here's a simile: Her teeth were like pearls. Everybody, say that. Get ready. (Signal.) *Her teeth were like pearls.*
- What are the two things that are the same? (Call on a student. Idea: *Her teeth and pearls.*)
- Now tell me how her teeth were like pearls. The teeth and pearls are the same in what way? (Call on a student. Ideas: *Both were shiny and white; both were sparkling white.*)

c. Here's another simile: Her eyes were as big as saucers. Everybody, say that. Get ready. (Signal.) *Her eyes were as big as saucers.*
- What are the two things that are the same? (Call on a student. Idea: *Her eyes and saucers.*)
- What's the same about her eyes and a saucer? (Call on a student. Idea: *Both are big and round.*)

d. Here's another simile: Uncle Charlie moved like a bear. Everybody, say that. (Signal.) *Uncle Charlie moved like a bear.*
- What are the two things that are the same? (Call on a student. Idea: *Uncle Charlie and a bear.*)
- What's the same about the way Uncle Charlie and a bear moved? (Call on a student. Ideas: *Both not graceful; both take heavy steps; both rock while walking.*)

e. Here's another simile: The palm of his hand was like sandpaper. Everybody, say that. Get ready. (Signal.) *The palm of his hand was like sandpaper.*
- What are the two things that are the same? (Call on a student. Idea: *The palm of his hand and sandpaper.*)
- What's the same about his hand and sandpaper? (Call on a student. Ideas: *Both feel scratchy; both are rough.*)

f. Find part A on your worksheet. ✔
   These are the similes we just went over.
   You'll answer the questions about each
   simile.

g. (Tell the students when they should
   complete the items in parts A and B.)

h. (After the students complete the items,
   do a workcheck. For each item: Read
   the item. Call on a student to answer it.
   If the answer is wrong, say the correct
   answer.)

Answer Key: Part A: 1. Her teeth and
pearls **2.** Ideas: Both were white and shiny;
both were sparkling white. **3.** Her eyes and
saucers **4.** Idea: Both are big and round.
5. Uncle Charlie and a bear. **6.** Ideas: Both
rock when they walk; both are not graceful;
both take heavy steps. **7.** (The palm of) his
hand and sandpaper **8.** Ideas: Both are
rough; both are scratchy.

Part B: 1. glistening—shining **2.** husky—big
and strong

SIMILES

Name _____

Lesson 115

A. Answer the questions.

1. What do we call expressions that use the words **like** or **as** and that tell about things that are the same? _____

   • He has eyes like a hawk.

2. What two things are the same? _____
3. How are they the same? _____

   • They work as hard as ants.

4. What two things are the same? _____
5. How are they the same? _____

   • She had a smile like sunshine.

6. What two things are the same? _____
7. How are they the same? _____

   • His muscles were as hard as rocks.

8. What two things are the same? _____
9. How are they the same? _____

B. Use your dictionary to find the correct meaning of the underlined word in each sentence. Circle the correct meaning.

1. We had <u>mullet</u> for dinner.
   • a vegetable   • a fish   • a fruit
2. His mother is an <u>aviator</u>.
   • pilot   • doctor   • nurse

BLM 58   179

a. You've worked with expressions that name two things that are the same. Everybody, what is that kind of expression called? (Signal.) *A simile.*

• Remember, a simile uses the word **like** or the word **as.** What words do similes use? (Signal.) *Like or as.*

b. Here's a simile: He has eyes like a hawk. Everybody, say that. Get ready. (Signal.) *He has eyes like a hawk.*

• What are the two things that are the same? (Call on a student. Idea: *His eyes and a hawk.*)

• What's the same about his eyes and a hawk? (Call on a student. Ideas: *Both are very sharp; both see very well.*)

c. Here's another simile: They work as hard as ants. Everybody, say that. Get ready. (Signal.) *They work as hard as ants.*

• What are the two things that are the same? (Call on a student. Idea: *They and ants.*)

• What's the same? (Call on a student. Idea: *Both work very hard.*)

d. Here's another simile: She had a smile like sunshine. Everybody, say that. Get ready. (Signal.) *She had a smile like sunshine.*

• What are the two things that are the same? (Call on a student. Idea: *Her smile and sunshine.*)

• What's the same about her smile and sunshine? (Call on a student. Ideas: *Both are bright; both are cheerful; both make you happy.*)

e. Here's another simile. His muscles were as hard as rocks. Everybody, say that. Get ready. (Signal.) *His muscles were as hard as rocks.*

• What are the two things that are the same? (Call on a student. Idea: *His muscles and rocks.*)

• What's the same about his muscles and rocks? (Call on a student. Idea: *Both are hard.*)

f. Find part A on your worksheet. ✔ These are the similes we just went over. You'll answer the questions.

g. (Tell the students when they should complete the items in parts A and B.)

h. (After the students complete the items, do a workcheck. For each item: Read the item. Call on a student to answer it. If the answer is wrong, say the correct answer.)

Answer Key: Part A: 1. Similes **2.** His eyes and a hawk **3.** Ideas: Both are sharp; both see very well. **4.** They and ants **5.** Idea: Both work very hard. **6.** Her smile and sunshine **7.** Ideas: Both are bright; both are cheerful; both make you happy. **8.** His muscles and rocks **9.** Idea: Both are hard.

Part B: 1. mullet—a fish **2.** aviator—pilot

Lesson 116

MEANING FROM CONTEXT

Name _____

Lesson 116

A.

A. Some of the people were very sad, but others were <u>elated</u>.

B. Her brother was very rich, but she was <u>impecunious</u>.

C. Bret's explanations were always clear, but Andy's explanations were always <u>ambiguous</u>.

Draw a line from each word in the first column to the word or words that mean the same thing.

1. impecunious •   • not clear

2. elated •   • poor

3. ambiguous •   • happy

B. Use your dictionary to find the correct meaning of the underlined word in each sentence. Circle the correct meaning.

1. My little sister can be very <u>mulish</u>.
   • cute   • happy   • stubborn

2. The teacher <u>revoked</u> their recess.
   • replaced   • took away   • gave away

180   BLM 59

a. Find part A on your worksheet. ✔

• Each sentence gives you information that helps you figure out the meaning of the underlined word.

b. Sentence A. Follow along. Some of the people were very sad, but others were elated. That tells about two things that are opposite; one of the opposites is **sad.**

• Everybody, what does the sentence tell you is the opposite of **sad?** (Signal.) *Elated.*

• So what does the word **elated** mean? (Signal.) *Happy.*

c. Sentence B also tells about opposites. Her brother was very rich, but she was impecunious.

• Everybody, what does the sentence tell you is the opposite of **rich?** (Signal.) *Impecunious.*

• So what does the word **impecunious** mean? (Signal.) *Poor.*

d. Sentence C also tells about opposites. Bret's explanations were always clear, but Andy's explanations were always ambiguous.

• Everybody, what does the sentence tell you is the opposite of **clear?** (Signal.) *Ambiguous.*

• So what does the word **ambiguous** mean? (Call on a student. Idea: *Not clear.*)

e. You'll draw a line from each word in the first column to the word or words that means the opposite.

f. (Tell the students when they should complete the items in parts A and B.)

g. (After the students complete the items, do a workcheck. For each item: Read the item. Call on a student to answer it. If the answer is wrong, say the correct answer.)

Answer Key: Part A: 1. poor **2.** happy **3.** not clear

Part B: 1. mulish—stubborn **2.** revoked—took away

Lesson 117

Materials: Each student will need a copy of the worksheet for lesson 117 (blackline master 60); the teacher and each student will need a copy of the same children's dictionary.

MEANING FROM CONTEXT

Name _____

Lesson 117

A.

A. The twins were not the same. One of them was very shy. The other was very <u>extroverted</u>.

B. Sometimes she was very thoughtful. At other times, she was <u>cavalier</u>.

C. Most of the time her voice was loud. But sometimes, her voice was <u>inaudible</u>.

Draw a line from each word in the first column to the word or words that mean the same thing.

1. inaudible •   • not thoughtful

2. extroverted •   • not shy

3. cavalier •   • soft

B. Use your dictionary to find the correct meaning of the underlined word in each sentence. Circle the correct meaning.

1. We could see fish in the <u>shoals</u>.
   • shallow water   • dirty water   • deep water

2. My dad planted a <u>poplar</u> in our yard.
   • a tree   • a shrub   • a flower

BLM 60   181

a. Find part A on your worksheet. ✔

• Each item gives you information that helps you figure out the meaning of the underlined word.

b. Item A. Follow along. The twins were not the same. One of them was very shy. The other was very extroverted.

• Everybody, what does the sentence tell you is the opposite of **shy?** (Signal.) *Extroverted.*

• So what does the word **extroverted** mean? (Call on a student. Ideas: *Not shy; sociable.*)

c. Item B also tells about opposites. Sometimes she was very thoughtful. At other times, she was cavalier.

• Everybody, what does the sentence tell you is the opposite of **thoughtful?** (Signal.) *Cavalier.*

• So what does the word **cavalier** mean? (Call on a student. Idea: *Not thoughtful.*)

d. Item C also tells about opposites. Most of the time her voice was loud. But sometimes, her voice was inaudible.

• Everybody, what does the sentence tell you is the opposite of **loud?** (Signal.) *Inaudible.*

• So what does the word **inaudible** mean? (Call on a student. Idea: *Soft.*)

e. You'll draw a line from each word in the first column to the word or words that means the opposite.

f. (Tell the students when they should complete the items in parts A and B.)

g. (After the students complete the items, do a workcheck. For each item: Read the item. Call on a student to answer it. If the answer is wrong, say the correct answer.)

Answer Key: Part A: 1. soft **2.** not shy **3.** not thoughtful

Part B: 1. shoals—shallow water **2.** poplar—a tree

Materials: Each student will need a copy of the worksheet for lesson 118 (blackline master 61); the teacher and each student will need a copy of the same children's dictionary.

MEANING FROM CONTEXT

Name _____

Lesson 118

A.

A. The boys had some money for the movie, and the girls also had some <u>currency</u>.

B. Jan was always careful when danger was near. Her brother was not as <u>cautious</u> as she was.

C. Bret's explanations were always very short. Bret's mother also gave explanations that were <u>terse</u>.

D. Some of the workers did not mind being poor, but others complained because they were so <u>indigent</u>.

Draw a line from each word in the first column to the word that is a synonym.

1. cautious •   • very short
2. indigent •   • careful
3. currency •   • money
4. terse •   • poor

B. Use your dictionary to find the correct meaning of the underlined word in each sentence. Circle the correct meaning.

1. The group walked toward the <u>portal</u> of the zoo.
   • exit   • center   • entrance

2. I <u>intend</u> to go to the movies tonight.
   • hope   • plan   • want

182 BLM 61

a. Find part A on your worksheet. ✔
• Each item gives you information that helps you figure out the meaning of the underlined word.
b. Item A. Follow along. The boys had some money for the movie, and the girls also had some currency.
• That sentence tells about two words that are synonyms. They mean the same thing.
• Everybody, what does the item tell you is a synonym for **money?** (Signal.) *Currency.*
c. Item B also tells about synonyms. Jan was always careful when danger was near. Her brother was not as cautious as she was.

• Everybody, what does the sentence tell you is a synonym for **careful?** (Signal.) *Cautious.*
d. Item C also tells about synonyms. Bret's explanations were always very short. Bret's mother also gave explanations that were terse.
• Everybody, what does the item tell you is a synonym for **short?** (Signal.) *Terse.*
e. Item D. Some of the workers did not mind being poor, but others complained because they were so indigent.
• Everybody, what does the sentence tell you is a synonym of **poor?** (Signal.) *Indigent.*
f. You'll draw a line from each word in the first column to the word that is a synonym.
g. (Tell the students when they should complete the items in parts A and B.)
h. (After the students complete the items, do a workcheck. For each item: Read the item. Call on a student to answer it. If the answer Is wrong, say the correct answer.)

Answer Key: Part A: 1. careful **2.** poor
3. money **4.** very short

Part B: 1. portal—entrance **2.** intend—plan

Lesson 119

INDEX

Name _____

Lesson 119

Write the first page in your textbook that tells about each topic.

1. Italy _____
2. circus _____
3. Japan _____
4. time _____
5. wooden buildings _____

Lesson 120

Write the first page in your textbook that tells about each topic.

1. kangaroos _____
2. parts of a ship _____
3. Australia _____
4. time machines _____
5. apostrophe _____

BLM 62   183

a. Find page 360 in your textbook. ✔
- This part of the book is the index. Everybody, what's this part called? (Signal.) *The index.*
- The index lists different topics that are in this book. The topics are listed alphabetically. One of the first topics is **Canada.** Touch that topic. **(Observe students and give feedback.)**

b. The index tells where you can read about Canada in this book. Touch the first page number for Canada. Everybody, what's the first page in this book that tells about Canada? (Signal.) *73.*
- Is that the only page that tells about Canada? (Signal.) *No.*

c. (Write on the board:)

134–138

- Sometimes, a topic in the book takes up more than one page. If the index showed the numbers on the board for a topic, the numbers would tell you that the topic starts on page 134 and it continues until page 138.

d. (Change the example to:)

96–98

- These numbers tell about a different topic that takes up more than one page. Everybody, on what page does this topic start? (Signal.) *96.*
- On what page does this topic end? (Signal.) *98.*
- (Touch the dash between the numbers.)
- Remember, if the numbers have a dash between them, they will tell about a topic that takes up more than one page.

e. Your turn. Look at the page numbers in the index and find the first place that shows a pair of numbers for a topic that takes more than one page. Raise your hand when you've done that much. **(Observe students and give feedback.)**
- Everybody, what's the name of the first topic that takes up more than one page? (Signal.) *Andy leaves the team.*
- On what page does that topic start? (Signal.) *23.*
- On what page does that topic end? (Signal.) *26.*

f. Find lesson 119 on your worksheet. ✔
- I'll read the directions. Write the first page in your textbook that tells about each topic. That means you'll write only **one** page number for each topic. That's the number of the **first** page where that topic appears in the book.

g. What's item 1? (Call on a student.) *Italy.*
• Everybody, write the first page number for that topic. Raise your hand when you've done that much.
  (Observe students and give feedback.)
• Everybody, what's the first page number for **Italy?** (Signal.) *47.*
h. (Tell the students when they should complete the items.)

i. (After the students complete the items, do a workcheck. For each item: Read the item. Call on a student to answer it. If the answer is wrong, say the correct answer.)

Answer Key: 1. 47 **2.** 129 **3.** 47 **4.** 112 **5.** 190

Lesson 120

Materials: Each student will need a copy of the worksheet for lesson 120 (blackline master 62) and a copy of textbook C.

INDEX
a. Find lesson 120 on your worksheet. ✔
• You'll write the first page in your textbook that tells about each topic. Everybody, what part of the book tells about where you'll find these topics? (Signal.) *The index.*
b. Look at the index and write the first page for topic 1. ✔
• Everybody, what's the first page number for **kangaroos?** (Signal.) *97.*

c. (Tell the students when they should complete the items.)
d. (After the students complete the items, do a workcheck. For each item: Read the item. Call on a student to answer it. If the answer is wrong, say the correct answer.)

Answer Key: 1. 97 **2.** 113 **3.** 88 **4.** 191 **5.** 184

Lesson 121

**Materials:** Each student will need a copy of the worksheet for lesson 121
(blackline master 63) and a copy of textbook C.

INDEX

Name _____

Lesson 121

1. You want to find the first page in the textbook that tells about
   contractions. On what page does that topic begin? _____
2. Write the first word on that page. _____
3. On what page does the topic end? _____
4. Write the last word on that page. _____
5. You want to find the first page in the textbook that tells about **England.**
   On what page does that topic begin? _____
6. Write the first word on that page. _____
7. On what page does the topic end? _____
8. Write the last word on that page. _____

a. Find lesson 121 on your worksheet. ✔

• I'll read what the first item says. You want to find the first page in the textbook that tells about **contractions.** On what page does that topic begin?

• You have to figure out where the topic begins. Everybody, what part of the book would you use to find out where the topic first appears? (Signal.) *The index.*

b. You're going to write the answer to item 1. Look up **contractions** in the index and write the first page where that topic appears.
   (Observe students and give feedback.)

• Everybody, on what page does the topic **contractions** appear? (Signal.) *184.*

c. Now you're going to copy words from the textbook. Go to the page of the textbook where **contractions** begins.
   (Students should turn to page 184.)
   (Observe students and give feedback.)

• Touch the first word on the page. ✔

• Everybody, what word is that? (Signal.) *Future.*

• That's the beginning word. Write that word on your worksheet for item 2. ✔

d. Now, look in the index and write the page number where the topic **contractions** ends for item 3.
   (Observe students and give feedback.)

• Everybody, on what page does the topic **contractions** end? (Signal.) *187.*

e. For item 4, go to the last page for the topic **contractions,** and write the last word on that page.
   (Observe students and give feedback.)

• Everybody, what's the last word? (Signal.) *End.*

f. Items 5 through 8 are like items 1 through 4. Look in the index and write the beginning page for the first time **England** appears in the textbook. Raise your hand when you've done that much.
   (Observe students and give feedback.)

• Everybody, on what page does the topic **England** first appear? (Signal.) *313.*

• Turn to the page where **England** first appears in the textbook and write the first word on that page. Raise your hand when you've done that much.
   (Observe students and give feedback.)

• Everybody, what's the first word on the page that tells about England? (Signal.) *August.*

• Everybody, on what page does the topic **England** end? (Signal.) *315.*

• Now go to the last page of the topic **England** and write the last word on that page.
   (Observe students and give feedback.)

• Everybody, what's the last word on the page that tells about England? (Signal.) *War.*

Lesson 122

Materials: Each student will need a copy of the worksheet for lesson 122 (blackline master 63) and a copy of textbook C.

INDEX

a. Find lesson 122 on your worksheet. ✔

• You're going to find out the first page where different topics appear in your textbook. Everybody, what part of the book would you use to find out where a topic first appears? **(Signal.)** *The index.*

b. For item 1, look up **city of the future** in the index and write the first page where that topic appears.
(Observe students and give feedback.)

• Everybody, on what page does the topic **city of the future** first appear? **(Signal.)** *267.*

c. Now you're going to copy words from the textbook. Go to the page of the textbook where the topic **city of the future** begins. **(Students should turn to page 267.)**
(Observe students and give feedback.)

• Touch the first word on that page. ✔

• Everybody, what word is that? **(Signal.)** *Dot.*

• That's the beginning word. Write that word on your worksheet for item 3. ✔

d. Now look in the index and write the page number where the topic **city of the future** ends.
(Observe students and give feedback.)

• Everybody, on what page does the topic end? **(Signal.)** *270.*

e. Now go to the last page of the topic **city of the future,** and write the last word on that page.
(Observe students and give feedback.)

• Everybody, what's the last word? **(Signal.)** *Time.*

f. Items 5 through 8 are like items 1 through 4. Look in the index and write the beginning page for the first time that **Columbus** appears in the textbook. Raise your hand when you've done that much.
(Observe students and give feedback.)

• Everybody, on what page does the topic **Columbus** appear? **(Signal.)** *277.*

• Turn to the page where **Columbus** first appears in the textbook and write the first word on that page. Raise your hand when you've done that much.
(Observe students and give feedback.)

• Everybody, what's the first word on the page that tells about Columbus? **(Signal.)** *Eric.*

g. Now look in the index and write the page number where the topic **Columbus** ends.
(Observe students and give feedback.)

• Everybody, on what page does the topic **Columbus** end? **(Signal.)** *297.*

• Now go to the last page of the topic **Columbus** and write the last word on that page.
(Observe students and give feedback.)

• Everybody, what's the last word on the page that tells about Columbus? **(Signal.)** *Side.*

Lesson **123**

INDEX

Name _____

Lesson 123

1. What part of the textbook gives an alphabetical listing of topics that appear in the book? _____

2. On what page does the topic **lion** first appear in the textbook? _____

3. Write the first word on that page. _____

4. On what page does the topic **lion** end? _____

5. Write the last word on that page. _____

Lesson 124

1. What part of the textbook gives an alphabetical listing of topics that appear in the book? _____

2. On what page does the topic **palace** first appear in the textbook? _____

3. Write the first word on that page. _____

4. On what page does the topic **palace** end? _____

5. Write the last word on that page. _____

a. (Tell the students when they should complete the items.)

b. (After the students complete the items, do a workcheck. For each item: Read the item. Call on a student to answer it. If the answer is wrong, say the correct answer.)

Answer Key: 1. index **2.** 246 **3.** just **4.** 252 **5.** teacher

Lesson **124**

INDEX

a. (Tell the students when they should complete the items.)

b. (After the students complete the items, do a workcheck. For each item: Read the item. Call on a student to answer it. If the answer is wrong, say the correct answer.)

Answer Key: 1. index **2.** 231 **3.** softly **4.** 241 **5.** time

Lesson 125

Materials: Each student will need a copy of the worksheet for lesson 125 (blackline master 65) and a copy of textbook C.

INDEX

a. (Tell the students when they should complete the items.)
b. (After the students complete the items, do a workcheck. For each item: Read the item. Call on a student to answer it. If the answer is wrong, say the correct answer.)

Answer Key: 1. index **2.** 47 **3.** look **4.** 51 **5.** outfit

Lesson 126

Materials: Each student will need a copy of the worksheet for lesson 126 (blackline master 65) and a copy of textbook C.

INDEX

a. (Tell the students when they should complete the items.)
b. (After the students complete the items, do a workcheck. For each item: Read the item. Call on a student to answer it. If the answer is wrong, say the correct answer.)

Answer Key: 1. Pacific Ocean: Hohoboho, present–day travel **2.** words with scars: Vikings, words with scars **3.** sailing ships: pyramids, United States

Lesson **127**

Materials: Each student will need a copy of the worksheet for lesson 127 (blackline master 66) and a copy of textbook C.

INDEX

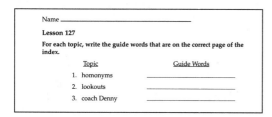

a. (Tell the students when they should complete the items.)

b. (After the students complete the items, do a workcheck. For each item: Read the item. Call on a student to answer it. If the answer is wrong, say the correct answer.)

Answer Key: 1. homonyms: Hohoboho, present–day travel **2.** lookouts: Hohoboho, present–day travel **3.** coach Denny: Andrew, Eric and Tom

Lesson 128

Materials: Each student will need a copy of the worksheet for lesson 128 (blackline master 66) and a copy of textbook C.

BOOK PARTS

Lesson 128

Write the name of the part of the book you would use for each item. The answer to each item is **glossary, index,** or **table of contents.**

1. You want to find out what selection starts on page 150.

2. You want to find out on what page the textbook first discusses Egypt.

3. You want to find out what the word **survive** means.

4. You want to find out how many reading selections are presented on lesson 132.

5. You want to find out the page number for the first selection on lesson 136.

6. You want to find out the first page number for the topic **earthquakes.**

7. You want to find the lesson number for the selection that starts on page 92 of your textbook.

BLM 66 187

a. You've learned about three parts of a book—the table of contents, the index, and the glossary.

b. Let's review. The glossary is at the end of your textbook. It tells the meaning of words that are introduced in the program. Everybody, what does the glossary tell? (Signal.) *The meaning of words introduced in the program.*

• The glossary lists these words alphabetically. Everybody, how are the words listed? (Signal.) *Alphabetically.*

c. The index is another alphabetical list. But it doesn't list words. It lists **topics.** Everybody, what does the index list? (Signal.) *Topics.*

• And how are the items listed? (Signal.) *Alphabetically.*

d. The table of contents is at the beginning of the book. It lists things by page number, not alphabetically.

• Everybody, which list is not alphabetical? (Signal.) *Table of contents.*

• Where do you find the table of contents? (Call on a student.) Idea: *At the front of the book.*

• The table of contents lists the selections that appear in the book. Everybody, what does the table of contents list? (Signal.) *The selections that appear in the book.*

e. Get ready to answer some questions. You want to find out the meaning of a word that appears in the program. Everybody, do you go to the glossary, the index, or the table of contents? (Signal.) *The glossary.*

• You want to find out what selection appears on lesson 122. Do you go to the glossary, the index, or the table of contents? (Signal.) *The table of contents.*

• You want to find the meaning of the word **magnetic.** Which list do you go to? (Signal.) *The glossary.*

• You want to find out all the places in the book that tell about the topic of Australia. Which list do you go to? (Signal.) *The index.*

• You want to find out what information passage appears on lesson 115. Which list do you go to? (Signal.) *The table of contents.*

• You want to find out where you can read about magnetism. Which list do you go to? (Signal.) *The index.*

f. Find lesson 128 on your worksheet. ✔ You're going to write the name of the part of the book you would use for each item. The answer for each item is glossary, index, or table of contents.

- Item 1 says: You want to find out what selection starts on page 150. Write the correct name.
  (Observe students and give feedback.)
- Everybody, what's the answer to item 1? (Signal.) *The table of contents.*

g. (Tell the students when they should complete the items.)

h. (After the students complete the items,

do a workcheck. For each item: Read the item. Call on a student to answer it. If the answer is wrong, say the correct answer.)

Answer Key: 1. table of contents **2.** index **3.** glossary **4.** table of contents **5.** table of contents **6.** index **7.** table of contents

Lesson 129

> **Materials:** Each student will need a copy of the worksheet for lesson 129 (blackline master 67) and a copy of textbook C.

BOOK PARTS

Name _____

Lesson 129

Write the name of the part of the book you would use for each item. The answer to each item is **glossary, index,** or **table of contents.**

1. You want to find out on how many pages the topic **King of Egypt** appears. _____

2. You want to find out the first page number for the topic **lookouts.** _____

3. You want to find out how many reading selections are presented on lesson 128. _____

4. You want to find out what the word **mention** means. _____

5. You want to find out the page number for the first selection on lesson 142. _____

6. You want to find out on what page the textbook first discusses **force.**
_____

188 *BLM 67*

a. (Tell the students when they should complete the items.)

b. (After the students complete the items, do a workcheck. For each item: Read the item. Call on a student to answer it. If the answer is wrong, say the correct answer.)

Answer Key: 1. index **2.** index **3.** table of contents **4.** glossary **5.** table of contents **6.** index

Materials: Each student will need a copy of the worksheet for lesson 130 (blackline master 68) and a copy of textbook C.

BOOK PARTS

Name _____

Lesson 130

Write the name of the part of the book you would use for each item. The answer to each item is glossary, index, or table of contents.

1. You want to find out the page number for the first selection on lesson 115. _____

2. You want to find out on what page the textbook first discusses **pyramids.** _____

3. You want to find out the first page number for the topic **homonyms.** _____

4. You want to find out what the word **shallow** means. _____

5. You want to find out how many reading selections are presented in lesson 124. _____

BLM 68 189

a. (Tell the students when they should complete the items.)

b. (After the students complete the items, do a workcheck. For each item: Read the item. Call on a student to answer it. If the answer is wrong, say the correct answer.)

Answer Key: **1.** table of contents **2.** index **3.** index **4.** glossary **5.** table of contents

Lesson 131

Materials: Each student will need a copy of the worksheet for lesson 131 (blackline master 69) and a copy of textbook C.

BOOK PARTS

Name _____

Lesson 131

Write the name of the part of the book you would use for each item. The answer to each item is **glossary, index, or table of contents.**

1. You want to find out on what page the textbook first discusses **platypus.** _____

2. You want to find out what the word **succeed** means. _____

3. You want to find out the lesson number for the selection that starts on page 85 of your textbook. _____

4. You want to find out the page number for the first selection on lesson 143. _____

5. You want to find out on how many pages the topic **Vikings** appears. _____

Lesson 132

For each item, write **glossary** or **index.** Then write the guide words that are on the correct page of the glossary or the index.

1. You want to find out on what page the textbook first discusses **building materials.** _____

2. You want to find out what the word **talent** means. _____

3. You want to find out on how many pages the topic **Italy** appears. _____

4. You want to find out what the word **warn** means. _____

190 BLM 69

a. (Tell the students when they should complete the items.)
b. (After the students complete the items, do a workcheck. For each item: Read the item. Call on a student to answer it. If the answer is wrong, say the correct answer.)

Answer Key: 1. index **2.** glossary **3.** table of contents **4.** table of contents **5.** index

Lesson 132

Materials: Each student will need a copy of the worksheet for lesson 132 (blackline master 69) and a copy of textbook C.

BOOK PARTS

a. (Tell the students when they should complete the items.)
b. (After the students complete the items, do a workcheck. For each item: Read the item. Call on a student to answer it. If the answer is wrong, say the correct answer.)

Answer Key: 1. index: Andrew, Eric, and Tom **2.** glossary: tackle, unpleasant **3.** index: Hohoboho, present–day travel **4.** glossary: usually, yard

Lesson **133**

Materials: Each student will need a copy of the worksheet for lesson 133 (blackline master 70) and a copy of textbook C.

BOOK PARTS

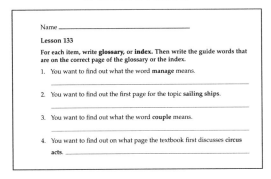

Name _____

Lesson 133

For each item, write **glossary**, or **index**. Then write the guide words that are on the correct page of the glossary or the index.

1. You want to find out what the word **manage** means.
_____

2. You want to find out the first page for the topic **sailing ships**.
_____

3. You want to find out what the word **couple** means.
_____

4. You want to find out on what page the textbook first discusses **circus acts**. _____

a. (Tell the students when they should complete the items.)

b. (After the students complete the items, do a workcheck. For each item: Read the item. Call on a student to answer it. If the answer is wrong, say the correct answer.)

Answer Key: 1. glossary: koala, measure **2.** index: pyramids, United States **3.** glossary: Columbus, damage **4.** index: Andrew, Eric, and Tom

Lesson **134**

Materials: Each student will need a copy of the worksheet for lesson 134 (blackline master 70) and a copy of textbook C.

BOOK PARTS

Lesson 134

Write the name of the part of the book you would use for each item. The answer to each item is **glossary, index, or table of contents**.

1. You want to find out what the word **preserve** means.
_____

2. You want to find out the lesson number for the selection that starts on page 195 of your textbook. _____

3. You want to find out on what page the textbook first discusses **Turkey**.
_____

4. You want to find out the first page number for the topic **future time**.
_____

5. You want to find out how many reading selections are presented on lesson 121. _____

BLM 70 191

a. (Tell the students when they should complete the items.)

b. (After the students complete the items, do a workcheck. For each item: Read the item. Call on a student to answer it. If the answer is wrong, say the correct answer.)

Answer Key: 1. glossary **2.** table of contents **3.** index **4.** index **5.** table of contents

Lesson **135**

Materials: Each student will need a copy of the worksheet for lesson 135 (blackline master 71) and a copy of textbook C.

BOOK PARTS

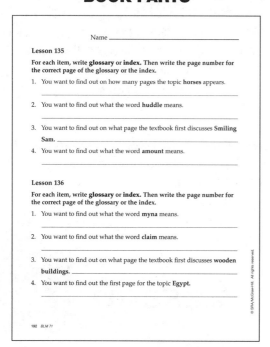

a. (Tell the students when they should complete the items.)
b. (After the students complete the items, do a workcheck. For each item: Read the item. Call on a student to answer it. If the answer is wrong, say the correct answer.)

Answer Key: 1. index: 362 **2.** glossary: 351 **3.** index: 363 **4.** glossary: 343

Lesson **136**

Materials: Each student will need a copy of the worksheet for lesson 136 (blackline master 71) and a copy of textbook C.

BOOK PARTS

a. (Tell the students when they should complete the items.)
b. (After the students complete the items, do a workcheck. For each item: Read the item. Call on a student to answer it. If the answer is wrong, say the correct answer.)

Answer Key: 1. glossary: 353 **2.** glossary: 345 **3.** index: 364 **4.** index: 360

Lesson 137

Materials: Each student will need a copy of the worksheet for lesson 137 (blackline master 72) and a copy of textbook C.

BOOK PARTS

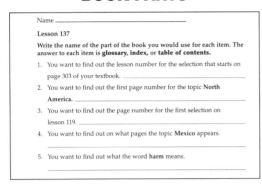

Name _____

Lesson 137

Write the name of the part of the book you would use for each item. The answer to each item is **glossary, index,** or **table of contents.**

1. You want to find out the lesson number for the selection that starts on page 303 of your textbook. _____

2. You want to find out the first page number for the topic **North America.** _____

3. You want to find out the page number for the first selection on lesson 119. _____

4. You want to find out on what pages the topic **Mexico** appears.
_____

5. You want to find out what the word **harm** means.
_____

a. (Tell the students when they should complete the items.)

b. (After the students complete the items, do a workcheck. For each item: Read the item. Call on a student to answer it. If the answer is wrong, say the correct answer.)

Answer Key: 1. table of contents **2.** index **3.** table of contents **4.** index **5.** glossary

Lesson 138

Materials: Each student will need a copy of the worksheet for lesson 138 (blackline master 72) and a copy of textbook C.

BOOK PARTS

Lesson 138

For each item, write **glossary** or **index.** Then write the page number for the correct page of the glossary or the index.

1. You want to find out what the word **during** means.
_____

2. You want to find out what the word **attach** means.
_____

3. You want to find out on what page the textbook first discusses **Italy.**
_____

4. You want to find out on how many pages the topic **Pip** appears.
_____

BLM 72   193

a. (Tell the students when they should complete the items.)

b. (After the students complete the items, do a workcheck. For each item: Read the item. Call on a student to answer it. If the answer is wrong, say the correct answer.)

Answer Key: 1. glossary: 347 **2.** glossary: 344 **3.** index: 362 **4.** index: 362

Lesson 139

Materials: Each student will need a copy of the worksheet for lesson 139 (blackline master 73) and a copy of textbook C.

BOOK PARTS

Name _____

Lesson 139

Write the name of the part of the book you would use for each item. The answer to each item is **glossary, index,** or **table of contents.**

1. You want to find out the page number for the first selection on lesson 125. _____

2. You want to find out on what page the textbook first discusses **cargo ship.** _____

3. You want to find out the first page number for the topic **time lines.** _____

4. You want to find out what the word **complaint** means. _____

5. You want to find out the lesson number for the selection that starts on page 245 of your textbook. _____

Lesson 140

For each item, write **glossary** or **index.** Then write the page number for the correct page of the glossary or the index.

1. You want to find out on how many pages the topic **Thrig** appears. _____

2. You want to find out what the word **rescue** means. _____

3. You want to find out on what page the textbook first discusses **cave people.** _____

4. You want to find out what the word **equipment** means. _____

194 *BLM 73*

a. (Tell the students when they should complete the items.)
b. (After the students complete the items, do a workcheck. For each item: Read the item. Call on a student to answer it. If the answer is wrong, say the correct answer.)

Answer Key: 1. table of contents **2.** index **3.** index **4.** glossary **5.** table of contents

Lesson 140

Materials: Each student will need a copy of the worksheet for lesson 140 (blackline master 73) and a copy of textbook C.

BOOK PARTS

a. (Tell the students when they should complete the items.)
b. (After the students complete the items, do a workcheck. For each item: Read the item. Call on a student to answer it. If the answer is wrong, say the correct answer.)

Answer Key: 1. index: 363 **2.** glossary: 355 **3.** index: 360 **4.** glossary: 348

Reproducible
Blackline Masters
Table of Contents

Name _____

Lesson 51

1. What part of your textbook shows a list of the selections in the book, starting with page 1? _____

2. What is the title of the selection for lesson 74? _____

   _____

3. On what page does the selection for lesson 74 begin? _____

4. What is the title of the selection for lesson 85? _____

5. On what page does that selection begin? _____

Lesson 52

1. How many selections are listed for lesson 84? _____

2. What's the title of the information passage? _____

3. What's the title of the story for lesson 84? _____

   _____

4. On what page does the story for lesson 84 begin? _____

   _____

5. What's the title for the selection that begins on page 173? _____

   _____

6. In which lesson does that selection appear? _____

Name —————————————————————————

Lesson 53

A. Write one or more than one after each sentence. Write jump or jumps in each blank.

1. The girl —————————————— . ————————————————

2. You and I —————————————— . ————————————————

3. Cats and dogs —————————— . ————————————————

4. Those frogs —————————————— . ————————————————

5. A man ——————————————————— . ————————————————

6. Mark and Henry ————————— . ————————————————

B.

1. How many selections are listed for lesson 81? ————————————————

2. What's the page number for the first selection in lesson 81? ——————

3. What's the page number for the second selection in lesson 81?

   ——

4. What's the title of the second selection? ————————————————

   ——

Lesson 54

A. Write one or more than one after each sentence. Write run or runs in each blank.

1. This woman _____. _____

2. Boys and girls _____. _____

3. She _____. _____

4. Her pals _____. _____

5. Her pal _____. _____

6. Two men _____. _____

B.

1. What's the lesson number for the selection that begins on page 91?

_____

2. What's the title of the selection that begins on page 91?

_____

3. What's the lesson number for the selection that begins on page 216?

_____

4. What's the title of the selection that begins on page 216?

_____

Name _____

Lesson 55

A. Write one or more than one after each sentence. Write hop or hops in each blank.

1. Joan and Barry _____ over logs. _____

2. She _____ over logs. _____

3. His dad and her mom _____ over logs. _____

4. This thin man _____ over logs. _____

B.

1. How many selections are listed for lesson 53? _____

2. What's the page number for the first selection in lesson 53?

   _____

3. What's the page number for the second selection in lesson 53?

   _____

4. What's the title of the second selection? _____

   _____

5. What's the title of the third selection? _____

   _____

Lesson 56

A. Write one or more than one after each sentence. Write sing or sings in each blank.

1. His dad _____ well. _____

2. His dad and mom _____ well. _____

3. Those ten kids _____ well. _____

4. Her older brothers _____ well. _____

B.

1. What's the lesson number for the selection that begins on page 374?

   _____

2. What's the title of the selection that begins on page 374?

   _____

3. What's the lesson number for the selection that begins on page 156?

   _____

4. What's the title of the selection that begins on page 156?

   _____

Name _____

Lesson 57

A. Write one or more than one after each sentence. Write talk or talks in each blank.

1. She _____ fast. _____

2. That rabbit _____ fast. _____

3. That rabbit and this skunk _____ fast. _____

4. Six bosses _____ fast. _____

B.

1. How many selections are listed for lesson 91? _____

2. What's the page number for the first selection in lesson 91? _____

3. What's the title of the first selection? _____

4. What's the page number for the second selection in lesson 91? _____

Lesson 58

1. What's the lesson number for the selection that begins on page 129?

    _____

2. What's the title of the selection that begins on page 129?

    _____

3. What's the lesson number for the selection that begins on page 328?

    _____

4. What's the title of the selection that begins on page 328?

    _____

Lesson 59

1. How many selections are listed for lesson 95? _____

2. What's the page number for the first selection in lesson 95? _____

3. What's the page number for the second selection in lesson 95?

   _____

4. What's the title of the second selection? _____

   _____

Lesson 60

1. What's the lesson number for the selection that begins on page 335?

   _____

2. What's the title of the selection that begins on page 335?

   _____

3. What's the lesson number for the selection that begins on page 55?

   _____

4. What's the title of the selection that begins on page 55?

   _____

Name _____

Lesson 61

great   visit

carrot   elephant

top   north

horse   jail

right   million

1. _____

2. _____

3. _____

4. _____

5. _____

6. _____

7. _____

8. _____

9. _____

10. _____

Lesson 62

length   forest

raise   yellow

bedroom   umbrella

should   desk

globe   whole

1. _____

2. _____

3. _____

4. _____

5. _____

6. _____

7. _____

8. _____

9. _____

10. _____

Name _____

Lesson 63

A. Write the missing part in each item.

1. Jim ran very fast, but Linda ran even _____.

2. All of the turtles are slow, but Amy's turtle is the _____.

3. Jan said to Al, "Let's go to the store." So Jan and Al _____.

4. There was a man in the room. Then another man walked into the room. So now there are two _____.

5. When I put my left foot in the tub, I had one wet foot. Then I put my right foot in the tub. So now I have two _____.

6. The more you cut a moop's hair, the faster its hair grows. Bob kept cutting his moop's hair, so that moop's hair _____.

B. Use the words below to make an alphabetical list.

only	monkey	1. _____
happen	baby	2. _____
answer	don't	3. _____
zoo	never	4. _____
house	perfect	5. _____
		6. _____
		7. _____
		8. _____
		9. _____
		10. _____

Name _____

Lesson 64

A. Write the missing part in each item.

1. Last week Ted lost a tooth. This week the same thing happened. So

   now Ted has _____.

2. At first one child was in the sandbox. Then another child came into the

   sandbox. Now there are _____ in the sandbox.

3. We have had some hot days this summer, but today is the _____
   day I can remember.

4. Jim said, "I will draw two pictures this week." And that is just what he

   did. He _____ two pictures.

5. In school, there were three turtles. Ed's turtle was four years old. Greg's

   turtle was five years old, so it was _____ than Ed's turtle. Bonnie's

   turtle was 14 years old, so it was the _____ turtle in school.

6. Joe told his mom he would sweep the sidewalk. He started to sweep
   the sidewalk when his sister asked him, "What are you doing?" Joe

   said, "I _____ ."

7. Henry had a loud voice. Tim spoke even _____ than Henry.

   Ernie spoke the _____ of all.

B. Use the words below to make an alphabetical list.

higher	unless	1. _____
tongue	funny	2. _____
ocean	question	3. _____
yourself	normal	4. _____
insect	knocked	5. _____
		6. _____
		7. _____
		8. _____
		9. _____
		10. _____

Name _____

Lesson 65

Use the words below to make an alphabetical list.

shovel	dance	1. _____
kitten	usually	2. _____
officer	lifeboat	3. _____
argued	half	4. _____
vacation	raindrop	5. _____
		6. _____
		7. _____
		8. _____
		9. _____
		10. _____

Lesson 66

Use the words below to make an alphabetical list.

label	unload	1. _____
enormous	decide	2. _____
rabbit	peaceful	3. _____
voice	middle	4. _____
captain	forever	5. _____
		6. _____
		7. _____
		8. _____
		9. _____
		10. _____

Lesson 67

A.

1. clothing

   A. _____

   B. _____

   C. _____

   D. _____

2. tools

   A. _____

   B. _____

   C. _____

   D. _____

3. vehicles

   A. _____

   B. _____

   C. _____

   D. _____

B.

⭐coat	🌙mirror	1. _____
climb	myna	2. _____
canned	metal	3. _____
curly	money	4. _____
crazy	machine	5. _____

Name _____

Lesson 68

A.

1. fruits

_____

_____

_____

_____

2. vegetables

_____

_____

_____

_____

3. animals

_____

_____

_____

_____

B. Underline the second letter in each word. Then write the words in alphabetical order.

oven	1. _____
once	2. _____
officer	3. _____
ocean	4. _____
outfit	5. _____

Lesson 69

A. containers   games   holidays

_____

    _____

    _____

    _____

    _____

_____

    _____

    _____

    _____

    _____

    _____

    _____

B. **Underline the second letter in each word. Then write the words in alphabetical order.**

swallow   second   1. _____   5. _____

squirrel   solid   2. _____   6. _____

steady   smelly   3. _____   7. _____

scale   shelves   4. _____   8. _____

Name _____

Lesson 70

A.   <u>**Things I Did**</u>

_____day   _____day   _____day

_____

_____

_____

_____

_____

_____

_____

_____

_____

_____

_____

_____

B. **All the words in the box begin with the letter B. Underline the second letter in each word. Then write the words in alphabetical order.**

boast	breath
building	beyond
blew	billows

1. _____   4. _____

2. _____   5. _____

3. _____   6. _____

Name _____

Lesson 71

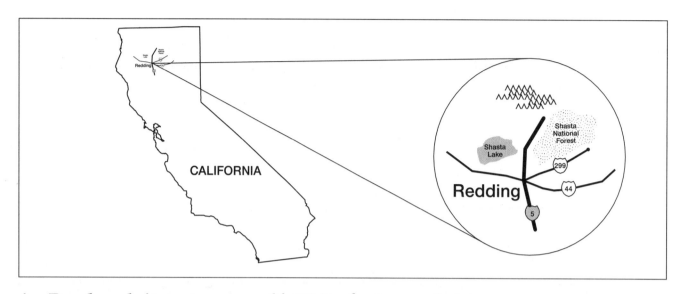

A. Read each item to yourself. Write fact or opinion.

1. Redding is a city in California. _____

2. Redding is the nicest place to live. _____

3. Redding is not one of the largest cities in California. _____

4. Redding is close to Shasta Lake. _____

5. Many tourists stop in Redding. _____

6. All other cities should try to be more like Redding. _____

7. There are mountains to the north of Redding. _____

8. Redding has great weather during all times of the year. _____

9. If you like places where there's a lot to do, you'll love Redding. _____

10. The trees around Redding are the best in the world. _____

11. There is a lot of farmland to the south of Redding. _____

12. Everybody you'll meet in Redding is very friendly. _____

Name _____

B. **All the words in the box below begin with the letter E. Underline the second letter in each word. Then write the words in alphabetical order.**

eraser	evening
enormous	escape
edge	eggs
easy	eyes

1. _____

2. _____

3. _____

4. _____

5. _____

6. _____

7. _____

8. _____

Lesson 72

A.

change	1. _____
cabbage	2. _____
dollar	3. _____
coast	4. _____
decide	5. _____
dream	6. _____
circus	7. _____

B. Read each item to yourself. Write fact or opinion.

1. Motorcycling is more fun than anything else. _____

2. Most new motorcycles cost more than $6000. _____

3. Motorcycles get better gas mileage than cars. _____

4. The best looking motorcycles are red. _____

5. Passengers on motorcycles are always comfortable. _____

6. When roads are icy or slippery, motorcycles may be dangerous. _____

7. Everybody who loves speed loves motorcycles. _____

Name _____

Lesson 73

A. Write about a person you respect.

Why I Respect ▌

A person I really respect is

(tell who) ▌.

I respect ▌ because

(tell why) ▌.

One time (tell something the person did that you respect)

▌

▌.

Another time (tell something else the person did that

you respect) ▌

▌.

I hope (tell what you hope about that person) ▌

▌.

Lesson 73

B. Here are rules for good manners when you're listening:

1. Look at the person who is talking.

2. Listen to what the person says.

3. Don't talk to your neighbors or make jokes while the person is talking.

4. Think about the parts that are good.

5. Think of what the person could do to make some of the parts better. Follow those rules and you'll become a really good listener.

C.

| trouble |
| thought |
| ruler |
| tenth |
| rich |
| twice |
| taste |
| rough |
| return |

1. _____

2. _____

3. _____

4. _____

5. _____

6. _____

7. _____

8. _____

9. _____

Name _____

Lesson 74

A.

middle	1. _____
island	2. _____
machine	3. _____
insist	4. _____
mummy	5. _____
money	6. _____
idea	7. _____

B. Write about places you would like to visit.

Places I Would Like To Visit

Places I would like to visit are _____ and _____ .

Here are the reasons I would like to visit _____ .

One reason is _____ .

Another reason is _____ .

Here are the reasons I would like to visit _____ .

One reason is _____ .

Another reason is _____ .

C. Here are rules for good manners when you're listening:

1. Look at the person who is talking.

2. Listen to what the person says.

3. Don't talk to your neighbors or make jokes while the person is talking.

4. Think about the parts that are good.

5. Think of what the person could do to make some of the parts better. Follow those rules and you'll become a really good listener.

Name _____

Lesson 75

A.

flower
juggle
football
fence
fifty
join

1. _____

2. _____

3. _____

4. _____

5. _____

6. _____

B. Write an interesting story about this picture.
- Tell what happened before the picture.
- Tell what happened in the picture.
- Tell what happened after the picture.
- You can write as many paragraphs as you want. Make your story interesting.

Lesson 76

A.

thirsty
notice
twice
terrible
neither
traffic
toast

1. _____

2. _____

3. _____

4. _____

5. _____

6. _____

7. _____

B. Write about a time you did something that you are proud of.

Something I Am Proud Of

I did something that I am proud

of (tell when) ████████████████ .

I was (tell where) ████████████ .

I was there because (tell why) ████████

████████████████ .

(Tell what happened. Tell what you did that you are proud of.

Tell all the important things.) ████████████

████████████████

Name _____

Lesson 77

A. Write an interesting story about this picture.
- Tell what happened before the picture.
- Tell what happened in the picture.
- Tell what happened after the picture.
- You can write as many paragraphs as you want. Make your story interesting.

B.

balloon	1. _____
lucky	2. _____
blood	3. _____
brave	4. _____
ledge	5. _____
busy	6. _____
liar	7. _____
bench	8. _____

Name _____

Lesson 78

A.

ruler	dinner
airplane	ceiling
done	report
knives	honest
thumb	weather

1. _____ 6. _____

2. _____ 7. _____

3. _____ 8. _____

4. _____ 9. _____

5. _____ 10. _____

B.

My Favorite Animal

My favorite animal is (tell what animal)

███████████████████████████████ .

Here are three things I really like about (tell what animal):

1. One thing I really like about (tell what animal) *is* ██████████████████ .

2. Another thing I really like about (tell what animal) *is* ███████████████ .

3. Another thing I really like about (tell what animal) *is* ███████████████ .

I hope (write what you hope about yourself and your favorite animal) ██████████████ .

Name _____

Lesson 79

A.

banana	1. _____
plastic	2. _____
electric	3. _____
people	4. _____
special	5. _____
early	6. _____
amaze	7. _____
hundred	8. _____
decide	9. _____
purple	10. _____

Name _____

Lesson 80

A.

shadow	great
lemon	younger
giant	bread
visit	space
destroy	globe

1. _____

2. _____

3. _____

4. _____

5. _____

6. _____

7. _____

8. _____

9. _____

10. _____

B.

What I Did Yesterday

Here are some of the things I did yesterday. (Tell about three or more things that you did yesterday.) ▮▮▮▮▮▮▮▮▮▮▮▮▮▮▮▮▮▮▮

Name —————————————————————————

Lesson 81

A.

count	cod
collar	coat
complete	cone
cob	cook

1. ——————————   5. ——————————

2. ——————————   6. ——————————

3. ——————————   7. ——————————

4. ——————————   8. ——————————

B. Write an interesting story about this picture.
- Tell what happened before the picture.
- Tell what happened in the picture.
- Tell what happened after the picture.
- You can write as many paragraphs as you want. Make your story interesting.

Name _____

Lesson 82

A.

dry	1. _____
driver	2. _____
draft	3. _____
dream	4. _____
drop	5. _____
drum	6. _____

B. _____

_____

_____

_____

_____

_____

_____

_____

_____

_____

_____

_____

Name _____

Lesson 83

A. Some word parts are called prefixes. Prefixes are the first part of some words. Some prefixes have a clear meaning.

Words	Opposites
1. agree	_____
2. appear	_____
3. like	_____
4. join	_____

B. Write an interesting story about this picture.
- Tell what happened before the picture.
- Tell what happened in the picture.
- Tell what happened after the picture.
- You can write as many paragraphs as you want. Make your story interesting.

Lesson 84

A.

1. arrange   _____

2. join   _____

3. appear   _____

4. charge   _____

B.

_____

_____

_____

_____

_____

_____

_____

_____

_____

_____

_____

_____

_____

_____

_____

Name _____

Lesson 85

A. Make a poem from this story.

STORY	POEM
There once was a <u>king</u>. Ring was his name.	• There once was a king
	_____
He always carried so much <u>gold</u> that he looked elderly.	• He always carried so much gold,
	_____
The gold was so heavy he couldn't stand up <u>tall</u>. Sometimes, he would have to crawl around.	• He couldn't stand up tall.
	_____
He was a terrible <u>sight</u>. He called in a doctor late one evening.	• He was a terrible sight.
	_____
The doctor said his problem was he was carrying too much gold with <u>him</u>. So he weighed a lot, even though he was a slim man.	• The doctor said the king had too much gold on him.
	_____
So the king left his gold at home after that <u>night</u>. And from then on, he could stand up the right way.	• The king left his gold at home after that night.
	_____
Now his face is full of <u>smiles</u>. He can walk a long, long way.	• Now his face is full of smiles.
	_____

Name _____

Lesson 85

B.   **1**   **2**   **3**

1. approve   _____   _____

2. arrange   _____   _____

3. order   _____   _____

4. join   _____   _____

5. connect   _____   _____

Lesson 86

  1   **2**   **3**

1. join   _____   _____

2. order   _____   _____

3. charge   _____   _____

4. connect   _____   _____

5. continue   _____   _____

Lesson 87

A. Write the word for each description.

1. What word means **to tell again?** _____

2. What word means **not able?** _____

3. What word means **not broken?** _____

4. What word means **to play again?** _____

5. What word means **the opposite of continue?** _____

6. What word means **not buttoned?** _____

Name _____

B. Make a poem from this story.

STORY	POEM
Cal was a big green <u>duck</u>. But Cal was not very lucky.	• Cal was a big green duck. _____
Things always went bad for <u>Cal</u>. Nobody wanted to be his friend.	• Things always went bad for Cal. _____
When Cal was around, things were never <u>good</u>. They never went the way they should go.	• When Cal was around, things were never good. _____
One day, there wasn't a cloud in the <u>sky</u>. As soon as Cal started to fly, clouds appeared all over.	• One day, there wasn't a cloud in the sky. _____
One duck said, "I'll make a <u>bet</u>. Before Cal lands, we'll all be covered with water."	• One duck said, "I'll make a bet. _____"
That duck was absolutely <u>right</u>. Everything was flooded before the night was over.	• That duck was absolutely right. _____

Lesson 88

A. Make a poem from this story.

STORY	POEM
Nearby lived a goose that the ducks learned to <u>hate</u>. They thought she was mean, but she thought she was good.	• Nearby lived a goose that the ducks learned to hate. _____
The ducks said to <u>Cal</u>, "See if you can make that goose your friend."	• The ducks said to Cal, "_____"
Cal went over to the goose and just said, "<u>Hi</u>." As he spoke, an eagle came out of the air.	• Cal went over to the goose and just said, "Hi." _____
The goose saw the eagle and flew far <u>away</u>. And the ducks never saw her after that time.	• The goose saw the eagle and flew far away. _____
Cal told the others, "I couldn't make that goose my <u>pal</u>." Those ducks said, "But now a lot of ducks really love you, buddy."	• Cal told the others, "I couldn't make that goose my pal." _____

Name _____

B. Write the word for each description.

1. What word means **the opposite of appear?** _____

2. What word means **to approve again?** _____

3. What word means **not clean?** _____

4. What word means **not fair?** _____

5. What word means **the opposite of connect?** _____

6. What word means **not aware?** _____

Lesson 89

Write the word for each description.

1. What word means **without effort?** _____

2. What word means **without a home?** _____

3. What word means **the opposite of order?** _____

4. What word means **to order again?** _____

5. What word means **not zipped?** _____

6. What word means **without a hat?** _____

Name _____

Lesson 90

Write the word for each description.

1. What word means **without trees?** _____

2. What word means **without form?** _____

3. What word means **to join again?** _____

4. What word means **the opposite of join?** _____

5. What word means **without joints?** _____

6. What word means **without clouds?** _____

Lesson 91

Write the word for each description.

1. What word means **full of harm?** _____

2. What word means **the opposite of charged?** _____

3. What word means **without thought?** _____

4. What word means **to think again?** _____

5. What word means **without care?** _____

6. What word means **full of care?** _____

Name _____

Lesson 92

Write the word for each description.

1. What word means **being hard?** _____

2. What word means **being tender?** _____

3. What word means **the opposite of belief?** _____

4. What word means **full of joy?** _____

5. What word means **without joy?** _____

6. What word means **being bright?** _____

7. What word means **not happy?** _____

8. What word means **without a shirt?** _____

Lesson 93

Write the word for each description.

1. What word means **to write again?** _____

2. What word means **being hard?** _____

3. What word means **the opposite of agree?** _____

4. What word means **not blinking?** _____

5. What word means **without hope?** _____

6. What word means **being fresh?** _____

7. What word means **being close?** _____

8. What word means **without a coat?** _____

Name _____

Lesson 94

Write the word for each description.

1. What word means **one who rides?** _____

2. What word means **being sad?** _____

3. What word means **full of thought?** _____

4. What word means **the opposite of approve?** _____

5. What word means **one who runs?** _____

6. What word means **without joy?** _____

7. What word means **being dull?** _____

8. What word means **not done?** _____

9. What word means **without sleeves?** _____

10. What word means **to read again?** _____

Name ────────────────────────────

Lesson 95

Write the word for each description.

1. What word means **to type again?** ─────────────

2. What word means **being cold?** ─────────────

3. What word means **to wash again?** ─────────────

4. What word means **one that washes?** ─────────────

5. What word means **one that bakes?** ─────────────

6. What word means **without taste?** ─────────────

7. What word means **full of skill?** ─────────────

8. What word means **being round?** ─────────────

9. What word means **without care?** ─────────────

10. What word means **one that tastes?** ─────────────

Name _____

Lesson 96

Write the word for each description.

1. What word means **being hard?** _____

2. What word means **very hard?** _____

3. What word means **being cold?** _____

4. What word means **very cold?** _____

5. What word means **the opposite of colored?** _____

6. What word means **to color again?** _____

7. What word means **full of tears?** _____

8. What word means **without tears?** _____

9. What word means **being bright?** _____

10. What word means **very bright?** _____

11. What word means **not healthy?** _____

Name _____

Lesson 97

Write the word for each description.

1. What word means **one that sits?** _____

2. What word means **being narrow?** _____

3. What word means **without pain?** _____

4. What word means **being firm?** _____

5. What word means **very firm?** _____

6. What word means **not firm?** _____

7. What word means **one that gives?** _____

8. What word means **to give again?** _____

9. What word means **without water?** _____

10. What word means **very fast?** _____

11. What word means **one that speaks?** _____

Name _____

Lesson 98

cents	cops
can	
certain	
cup	
chip	
circus	
clipper	
call	
city	

1. _____

2. _____

3. _____

4. _____

5. _____

Lesson 99

chief	clean
circle	
chill	
chew	
chirp	
copy	
chin	
chunk	
class	
claw	

1. _____

2. _____

3. _____

4. _____

5. _____

6. _____

7. _____

Name _____

Lesson 100

Use the glossary in your book to answer the questions.

1. What are the guide words for the word **slight?** _____

2. What are the guide words for the word **crouch?** _____

Lesson 101

camp	cell

cent	change

chap	chat

cheap	chop

1. cat _____

2. chest _____

3. chart _____

4. care _____

5. chair _____

6. chase _____

Lesson 102

<u>face</u>	<u>fasten</u>

<u>favorite</u>	<u>field</u>

<u>figure</u>	<u>first</u>

<u>five</u>	<u>float</u>

<u>foam</u>	<u>freeze</u>

<u>friend</u>	<u>frost</u>

1. frond   _____
2. fever   _____
3. famous   _____
4. flea   _____
5. factory   _____
6. finally   _____
7. forest   _____
8. faint   _____
9. frisky   _____
10. finish   _____

Name _____

Lesson 103

<u>label</u>	<u>lawyer</u>

<u>lazy</u>	<u>lifeboat</u>

<u>lightning</u>	<u>living</u>

<u>loaf</u>	<u>maggot</u>

<u>magic</u>	<u>matter</u>

<u>mean</u>	<u>meter</u>

1. metal _____
2. list _____
3. ledge _____
4. machine _____
5. lady _____
6. manage _____
7. learn _____
8. laughter _____
9. league _____
10. lucky _____

Name _____

Lesson 104

A. **For each word, underline the prefix. Circle the root. Make a line over the suffix.**

1. return
2. baker
3. superclean

4. brightness
5. disappear
6. recliner

B. **For each item, write the guide words that are on the correct page of the glossary in your textbook.**

<u>Word</u>   <u>Guide Words</u>

1. engine   _____

2. adventure   _____

3. gust   _____

Name _____

Lesson 105

A. For each word, underline the prefix. Circle the root. Make a line over the suffix.

1. helpful

2. result

3. retain

4. contain

5. disable

6. unhappiness

7. sustainable

B. For each item, write the guide words that are on the correct page of the glossary in your textbook.

Word	Guide Words
1. constantly	_____
2. imitate	_____
3. mention	_____

Lesson 106

A. For each word, underline the prefix. Circle the root. Make a line over the suffix.

1. subjective

2. injection

3. detainment

4. reject

5. projection

6. revert

7. inverted

B. For each item, write the guide words that are on the correct page of the glossary in your textbook.

Word	Guide Words
1. drifts	_____
2. occasional	_____
3. cargo	_____

Name _____

Lesson 107

A. For each word, underline the prefix. Circle the root. Make a line over the suffix.

1. produce

2. reply

3. implicate

4. compliance

5. diverting

6. supplier

7. reducing

B. For each item, write the guide words that are on the correct page of the glossary in your textbook.

Word   Guide Words

1. frequently   _____

2. approach   _____

3. magnet   _____

Name _____

Lesson 108

1. **descend**   They will <u>descend</u> the hill.

                                               • go up   • go down   • eat

2. **harrow**   The farmer came home with an old <u>harrow</u>.

                    • an animal   • a tool   • a person

3. **lavish**   Her house was very <u>lavish</u>.

      • small   • large   • more than someone needs

Lesson 109

1. **macaw**   They saw a <u>macaw</u> in the jungle.

      • a large tree   • a colorful bird   • a kind of pond

2. **oddment**   They had a lot of <u>oddments</u> after they finished the dinner.

      • stomach pains   • dirty dishes   • leftover food

3. **raiment**   Their <u>raiment</u> was stolen.

      • luggage   • clothing   • animals

Name _____

Lesson 110

1. **sanction**   The mayor <u>sanctioned</u> our plan.

    • approved of   • fought   • paid no attention to

2. **velocity**   The plane had a lot of <u>velocity</u>.

    • fuel   • passengers   • speed

3. **diminutive** His daughter was quite <u>diminutive</u>.

    • small   • quiet   • pretty

Lesson 111

Use your dictionary to find the correct meaning of the underlined word in each sentence. Circle the correct meaning.

1. She did not <u>deduct</u> the correct amount.

    • take away   • add   • change

2. She collected three <u>granules</u> of sand.

    • bags   • cups   • grains

Name _____

Lesson 112

A. Draw a line from each expression to what it means.

1. She slept like a log last night. •   • She was tough.

2. She was really hard nosed. •   • She talked a lot.

3. Well, I'll be a monkey's uncle. •   • She slept very soundly.

4. She talked until she
   was blue in the face. •   • The person was really
                                              surprised.

B. Use your dictionary to find the correct meaning of the underlined word in each sentence. Circle the correct meaning.

1. Her grandfather had large <u>jowls</u>.

   • bumps on hands   • bags under jaw   • stains on books

2. Sarah bought a <u>bassoon</u>.

   • fish   • musical instrument   • expensive stone

Name _____

Lesson 113

A. Draw a line from each expression to what it means.

1. He was always
   walking on thin ice. •

2. It was raining cats and dogs. •

3. He was really hard nosed. •

4. He could have been
   knocked over by a feather. •

5. He slept like a log. •

6. He always does best when
   his back is against the wall. •

• He was tough.

• He was really surprised.

• He slept very soundly.

• He does best when he
  faces serious problems.

• He was always doing
  dangerous things.

• It was raining very
  hard.

B. Use your dictionary to find the correct meaning of the underlined word in each sentence. Circle the correct meaning.

1. She emptied the bucket of <u>cinders</u>.

   • small bits of gravel   • clumps of dirt   • partly burned material

2. The <u>expenses</u> for the party were too much.

   • tickets   • costs   • presents

Lesson 114

A. Answer the questions about each simile.

- **Her teeth were like pearls.**

1. What two things are the same? _____

2. How were her teeth like pearls? _____

- **Her eyes were as big as saucers.**

3. What two things are the same? _____

4. What's the same about her eyes and saucers?

_____

- **Uncle Charlie moved like a bear.**

5. What two things are the same? _____

6. What's the same about the way Uncle Charlie and a bear moved?

_____

- **The palm of his hand was like sandpaper.**

7. What two things are the same? _____

8. What's the same about his hands and sandpaper?

_____

B. Use your dictionary to find the correct meaning of the underlined word in each sentence. Circle the correct meaning.

1. The snow was <u>glistening</u> in the sunlight.

  • shining   • melting   • falling

2. Three <u>husky</u> men took a nap.

  • tired   • tall and thin   • big and strong

Name _____

Lesson 115

A. Answer the questions.

1. What do we call expressions that use the words **like** or **as** and that tell about things that are the same? _____

   - **He has eyes like a hawk.**

2. What two things are the same? _____

3. How are they the same? _____

   - **They work as hard as ants.**

4. What two things are the same? _____

5. How are they the same? _____

   - **She had a smile like sunshine.**

6. What two things are the same? _____

7. How are they the same? _____

   - **His muscles were as hard as rocks.**

8. What two things are the same? _____

9. How are they the same? _____

B. Use your dictionary to find the correct meaning of the underlined word in each sentence. Circle the correct meaning.

1. We had <u>mullet</u> for dinner.

   - a vegetable   • a fish   • a fruit

2. His mother is an <u>aviator</u>.

   - pilot   • doctor   • nurse

Lesson 116

A.

A. Some of the people were very sad, but others were <u>elated</u>.

B. Her brother was very rich, but she was <u>impecunious</u>.

C. Bret's explanations were always clear, but Andy's explanations were always <u>ambiguous</u>.

Draw a line from each word in the first column to the word or words that mean the same thing.

1. impecunious •   • not clear

2. elated •   • poor

3. ambiguous •   • happy

B. Use your dictionary to find the correct meaning of the underlined word in each sentence. Circle the correct meaning.

1. My little sister can be very <u>mulish</u>.

   • cute   • happy   • stubborn

2. The teacher <u>revoked</u> their recess.

   • replaced   • took away   • gave away

Name _____

Lesson 117

A.

A. The twins were not the same. One of them was very shy. The other was very <u>extroverted</u>.

B. Sometimes she was very thoughtful. At other times, she was <u>cavalier</u>.

C. Most of the time her voice was loud. But sometimes, her voice was <u>inaudible</u>.

Draw a line from each word in the first column to the word or words that mean the same thing.

1. inaudible •   • not thoughtful

2. extroverted •   • not shy

3. cavalier •   • soft

B. Use your dictionary to find the correct meaning of the underlined word in each sentence. Circle the correct meaning.

1. We could see fish in the <u>shoals</u>.

   • shallow water   • dirty water   • deep water

2. My dad planted a <u>poplar</u> in our yard.

   • a tree   • a shrub   • a flower

Lesson 118

A.

A. The boys had some money for the movie, and the girls also had some <u>currency</u>.

B. Jan was always careful when danger was near. Her brother was not as <u>cautious</u> as she was.

C. Bret's explanations were always very short. Bret's mother also gave explanations that were <u>terse</u>.

D. Some of the workers did not mind being poor, but others complained because they were so <u>indigent</u>.

Draw a line from each word in the first column to the word that is a synonym.

1. cautious •   • very short

2. indigent •   • careful

3. currency •   • money

4. terse •   • poor

B. Use your dictionary to find the correct meaning of the underlined word in each sentence. Circle the correct meaning.

1. The group walked toward the <u>portal</u> of the zoo.

    • exit   • center   • entrance

2. I <u>intend</u> to go to the movies tonight.

    •hope   • plan   • want

Name _____

Lesson 119

Write the first page in your textbook that tells about each topic.

1. Italy _____

2. circus _____

3. Japan _____

4. time _____

5. wooden buildings _____

Lesson 120

Write the first page in your textbook that tells about each topic.

1. kangaroos _____

2. parts of a ship _____

3. Australia _____

4. time machines _____

5. apostrophe _____

Name _____

Lesson 121

1. You want to find the first page in the textbook that tells about **contractions.** On what page does that topic begin? _____

2. Write the first word on that page. _____

3. On what page does the topic end? _____

4. Write the last word on that page. _____

5. You want to find the first page in the textbook that tells about **England.** On what page does that topic begin? _____

6. Write the first word on that page. _____

7. On what page does the topic end? _____

8. Write the last word on that page. _____

Lesson 122

1. You want to find the first page in the textbook that tells about **city of the future.** On what page does that topic begin? _____

2. Write the first word on that page. _____

3. On what page does the topic end? _____

4. Write the last word on that page. _____

5. You want to find the first page in the textbook that tells about **Columbus.** On what page does that topic begin? _____

6. Write the first word on that page. _____

7. On what page does the topic end? _____

8. Write the last word on that page. _____

Name ———————————————————————————

Lesson 123

1. What part of the textbook gives an alphabetical listing of topics that appear in the book? ————————————————————————

2. On what page does the topic **lion** first appear in the textbook?

   ————————————————————————————

3. Write the first word on that page. ————————————————————

4. On what page does the topic **lion** end? ————————————————

5. Write the last word on that page. —————————————————————

Lesson 124

1. What part of the textbook gives an alphabetical listing of topics that appear in the book? ————————————————————————

2. On what page does the topic **palace** first appear in the textbook?

   ————————————————————————————

3. Write the first word on that page. ————————————————————

4. On what page does the topic **palace** end? ————————————————

5. Write the last word on that page. —————————————————————

Name _____

Lesson 125

1. What part of the textbook gives an alphabetical listing of topics that

   appear in the book? _____

2. On what page does the topic **Turkey** first appear in the textbook?

   _____

3. Write the first word on that page. _____

4. On what page does the topic **Turkey** end? _____

5. Write the last word on that page. _____

Lesson 126

For each topic, write the guide words that are on the correct page of the index.

Topic	Guide Words
1. Pacific Ocean	_____
2. words with scars	_____
3. sailing ships	_____

Name _____

Lesson 127

For each topic, write the guide words that are on the correct page of the index.

Topic	Guide Words
1. homonyms	_____
2. lookouts	_____
3. coach Denny	_____

Lesson 128

Write the name of the part of the book you would use for each item. The answer to each item is glossary, index, or table of contents.

1. You want to find out what selection starts on page 150.

   _____

2. You want to find out on what page the textbook first discusses Egypt.

   _____

3. You want to find out what the word **survive** means.

   _____

4. You want to find out how many reading selections are presented on

   lesson 132. _____

5. You want to find out the page number for the first selection on lesson

   136. _____

6. You want to find out the first page number for the topic **earthquakes.**

   _____

7. You want to find the lesson number for the selection that starts on page

   92 of your textbook. _____

Lesson 129

Write the name of the part of the book you would use for each item. The answer to each item is glossary, index, or table of contents.

1. You want to find out on how many pages the topic **King of Egypt** appears. _____

2. You want to find out the first page number for the topic **lookouts.**

   _____

3. You want to find out how many reading selections are presented on lesson 128. _____

4. You want to find out what the word **mention** means.

   _____

5. You want to find out the page number for the first selection on lesson 142. _____

6. You want to find out on what page the textbook first discusses **force.**

   _____

Name _____

Lesson 130

Write the name of the part of the book you would use for each item. The answer to each item is glossary, index, or table of contents.

1. You want to find out the page number for the first selection on

   lesson 115. _____

2. You want to find out on what page the textbook first discusses

   pyramids. _____

3. You want to find out the first page number for the topic **homonyms.**

   _____

4. You want to find out what the word **shallow** means.

   _____

5. You want to find out how many reading selections are presented in

   lesson 124. _____

Lesson 131

Write the name of the part of the book you would use for each item. The answer to each item is glossary, index, or table of contents.

1. You want to find out on what page the textbook first discusses

    platypus. _____

2. You want to find out what the word **succeed** means.

    _____

3. You want to find out the lesson number for the selection that starts on

    page 85 of your textbook. _____

4. You want to find out the page number for the first selection on

    lesson 143. _____

5. You want to find out on how many pages the topic **Vikings** appears.

    _____

Lesson 132

For each item, write glossary or index. Then write the guide words that are on the correct page of the glossary or the index.

1. You want to find out on what page the textbook first discusses

    building materials. _____

2. You want to find out what the word **talent** means.

    _____

3. You want to find out on how many pages the topic **Italy** appears.

    _____

4. You want to find out what the word **warn** means.

    _____

Name _____

Lesson 133

For each item, write glossary, or index. Then write the guide words that are on the correct page of the glossary or the index.

1. You want to find out what the word **manage** means.

   _____

2. You want to find out the first page for the topic **sailing ships**.

   _____

3. You want to find out what the word **couple** means.

   _____

4. You want to find out on what page the textbook first discusses **circus acts**. _____

Lesson 134

Write the name of the part of the book you would use for each item. The answer to each item is glossary, index, or table of contents.

1. You want to find out what the word **preserve** means.

   _____

2. You want to find out the lesson number for the selection that starts on page 195 of your textbook. _____

3. You want to find out on what page the textbook first discusses **Turkey.**

   _____

4. You want to find out the first page number for the topic **future time.**

   _____

5. You want to find out how many reading selections are presented on lesson 121. _____

Lesson 135

For each item, write glossary or index. Then write the page number for the correct page of the glossary or the index.

1. You want to find out on how many pages the topic **horses** appears.

    _____

2. You want to find out what the word **huddle** means.

    _____

3. You want to find out on what page the textbook first discusses **Smiling Sam.** _____

4. You want to find out what the word **amount** means.

    _____

Lesson 136

For each item, write glossary or index. Then write the page number for the correct page of the glossary or the index.

1. You want to find out what the word **myna** means.

    _____

2. You want to find out what the word **claim** means.

    _____

3. You want to find out on what page the textbook first discusses **wooden buildings.** _____

4. You want to find out the first page for the topic **Egypt.**

    _____

Name _____

Lesson 137

Write the name of the part of the book you would use for each item. The answer to each item is glossary, index, or table of contents.

1. You want to find out the lesson number for the selection that starts on page 303 of your textbook. _____

2. You want to find out the first page number for the topic **North America.** _____

3. You want to find out the page number for the first selection on lesson 119. _____

4. You want to find out on what pages the topic **Mexico** appears.

   _____

5. You want to find out what the word **harm** means.

   _____

Lesson 138

For each item, write glossary or index. Then write the page number for the correct page of the glossary or the index.

1. You want to find out what the word **during** means.

   _____

2. You want to find out what the word **attach** means.

   _____

3. You want to find out on what page the textbook first discusses **Italy.**

   _____

4. You want to find out on how many pages the topic **Pip** appears.

   _____

Lesson 139

Write the name of the part of the book you would use for each item. The answer to each item is glossary, index, or table of contents.

1. You want to find out the page number for the first selection on lesson 125. _____

2. You want to find out on what page the textbook first discusses **cargo ship.** _____

3. You want to find out the first page number for the topic **time lines.**

    _____

4. You want to find out what the word **complaint** means.

    _____

5. You want to find out the lesson number for the selection that starts on page 245 of your textbook. _____

Lesson 140

For each item, write glossary or index. Then write the page number for the correct page of the glossary or the index.

1. You want to find out on how many pages the topic **Thrig** appears.

    _____

2. You want to find out what the word **rescue** means.

    _____

3. You want to find out on what page the textbook first discusses **cave people.** _____

4. You want to find out what the word **equipment** means.

    _____